the ultimate guide to
clearing your clutter

the ultimate guide to
clearing your clutter

liberate your space, clear your mind, and bring in success

mary lambert

CICO BOOKS
LONDON NEW YORK

Published in 2010 by CICO Books
an imprint of Ryland Peters & Small
519 Broadway, 5th Floor, New York NY 10012
20–21 Jockey's Fields, London WC1R 4BW

www.cicobooks.com

10 9 8 7 6 5 4 3 2 1

Text copyright © Mary Lambert 2010
Design and illustrations copyright © CICO Books 2010
See page 175 for photography credits.

A CIP catalog record for this book is available from the Library of Congress
and the British Library.

ISBN: 978-1-907030-13-0

Printed in China

Editor: Liz Dean
Design: Roger Daniels and Paul Wood
Picture research: Gabrielle Allen
Illustration: Sam Wilson (pp 5, 13, 14, 19, 22, 30, 36, 37, 43, 48, 49,
55, 58, 59, 64, 65, 73, 79, 84, 86), Kate Simunek (pp 8, 24, 30, 34,
35, 40, 41, 47, 52, 56, 57, 62, 63, 69, 76, 77, 82, 83), and Trina
Dalziel (pp 98–176)

Note: In many instances in this book, we recommend that you clear out
financial paperwork regularly. However, bear in mind that in accordance
with standard financial practice in the UK, financial records, particularly
those relating to bank accounts, the Inland Revenue, and council tax,
should be kept for at least seven years.

The content of this book was previously published in the following titles:
Clearing the Clutter by Mary Lambert (CICO Books, 2001, ISBN: 978-1-
903116-13-5/Barnes & Noble Books, 2001, ISBN: 978-0-760722-03-9)
The Declutter Workbook by Mary Lambert (CICO Books, 2004, ISBN: 978-1-
903116-88-3/Barnes & Noble Books, 2003, ISBN: 978-0-760752-24-1)

Contents

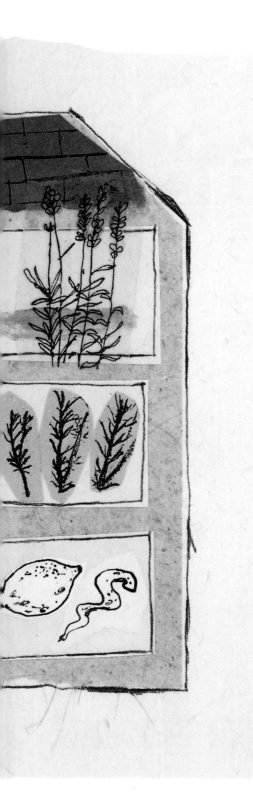

Introduction

An accumulation of clutter in our homes is something we all suffer from, but it is whether we manage to keep it under control or whether it starts to control us that is important. Feng shui is the ancient Chinese practice of furniture placement and energy flow in the home. Improving the flow of energy and creating good feng shui can bring about better health and increased prosperity and personal success. To achieve good feng shui in the home environment, it is first essential to clear out clutter. This is a powerful process that cleanses the space, helping to bring about amazing changes in the occupants' lives.

A major part of feng shui is controlling the flow of chi (energy) in the home. When chi enters the home and encounters obstructions, it slows down. Piles of clutter in a home create blockages that restrict the flow of chi, making it sluggish, and this has a detrimental effect on the occupants. The trouble is that once clutter starts to build up, it attracts more, and before you know it your home is a clutter nightmare. The sticky, slow energy that surrounds your junk makes you feel reluctant to progress in every area of your life, influencing you mentally, emotionally, and spiritually.

A NEW LIFE

Hanging onto too many old possessions keeps us linked to our past, and does not allow us to move on. The aim of *The Ultimate Guide to Clearing your Clutter* is to help you begin the process of clearing out these old possessions, because the longer you leave it, the harder it is to start.

Part one, Clearing the Clutter, Room by Room, explains why you are hoarding junk and how your life will change when you dispose of it, a little at a time. The major "clutter zones" in your home are identified, along with checklists and clutter-busting ideas. When your home is junk-free, there are plenty of ideas on boosting chi, as well as using feng shui enhancements such as water features, plants, and crystals.

Part two, The Declutter Projects, is entirely project-based. It takes you through all the rooms in your home, plus the yard or garden, and details specific clutter-clearing tasks to tackle. Each task is timed so that you can choose your tasks according to how much time you have. Toward the end of part two, there is a notebook section (see pages 148–171) where your drawing skills are needed. Questionnaires test you on any clutter overload you may have, while

sample room plans highlight how typical energy flow is obstructed by clutter.

Finally, we all need rewards for our efforts to de-junk our lives—so for every room you'll find a list of clear-out treats and a "wish card" to fill in (see page 176). Photocopy it on different colored papers, and display it as you go through the transformation process. By imagining your dream room, you take a step toward making it a reality.

The possessions that you keep in the kitchen need to be thought about carefully as in every other area of the home.

After attacking the relevant tasks, streamlining your home, and removing things that are no longer needed, you will create a place that nurtures and embraces you. You will find out what you really want in life, and allow space for new people and exciting opportunities to enter.

part one

clearing the clutter, room by room

You Are Your Clutter!

Clutter clearing is a powerful process that will bring startling changes in your life. Don't add crystals and other feng shui enhancements until you have tackled your clutter, because they just will not work.

In cluttered areas of your home, chi (energy) stagnates, and once this stale energy has accumulated, it will grow even more. Junk mail, abandoned craft projects, and newspapers waiting for recycling all constitute clutter. All those neglected items that you hide in corners, thinking you will make a decision about them later—but you never do—are clutter, too. Avoiding a drastic clear-out can stem from a fear of the future, but once you commit to it, you will move on and change.

YOUR INNER SOUL

Your home is supposed to mirror your inner self, so mess and inactivity reflects something that is going on inside of you. The chaos will also make you feel lethargic, stultified, and confused about what you want in your life. Once you have emptied out your junk hoard, you will feel physically, emotionally, and spiritually liberated, and you will find that you have opened the door to wonderful new opportunities.

What clearing out means

If your clutter is getting you down and you want to start getting rid of it, you are ready to make changes in your life to bring yourself closer to what you want. Don't underestimate the effects a clear-out can have on you. You may find it painful to get rid of possessions that you have kept for a long, long time, and feel that you cannot exist without them, even though an inner voice is telling you to let go. Once you have done this, you need to evaluate honestly what is relevant to your life now and in the future.

Think positively: saying that you feel you will be happier when the clutter is gone is not enough. Make a list of short-term and long-term goals, such as changing careers, starting a new business, having more free time for artistic pursuits, creating an area for hobbies, or embarking on a new relationship. Setting goals makes de-junking easier, because you are mentally clearing the pathway to your dreams.

You will feel much happier in yourself when you have cleared out rooms such as the bedroom and installed good storage units.

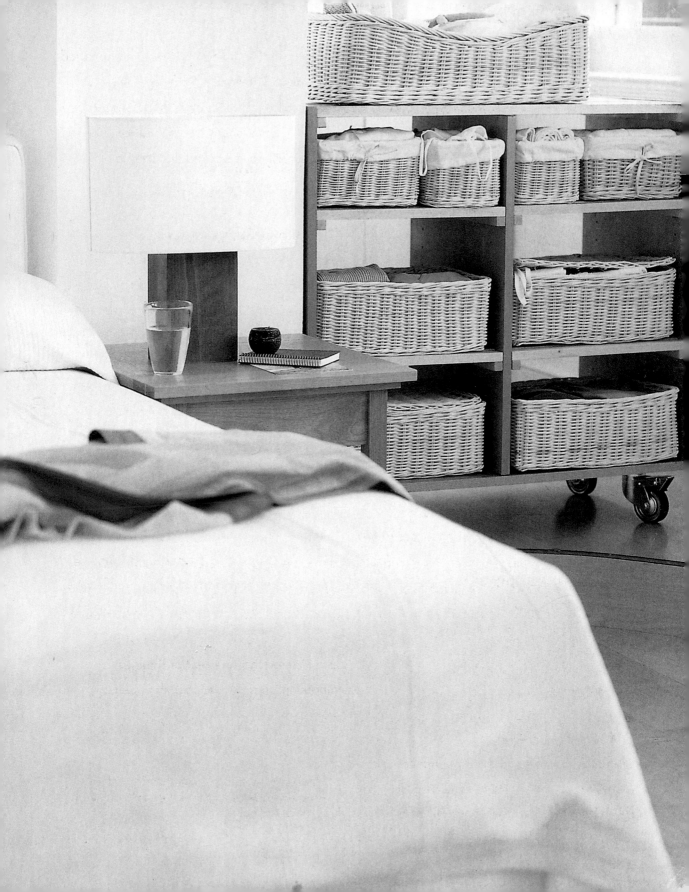

The flow of chi

According to the Chinese view of the universe, there is an invisible life force or energy, called chi, that flows through all things. Manipulating and balancing the flow of chi in the home is a major part of feng shui practice. When chi moves freely, the atmosphere is bright, charged, and uplifting.

The chi that flows through the home needs to have a strong movement in order to have a positive and beneficial impact on all the people who live there. It enters through the front door and then meanders through the rooms in a spiraling movement (see right), finding an exit through a back door and windows.

Clutter is the biggest obstacle to a smooth flow of chi, because it creates a blockage that chi cannot easily get around. When this occurs in the porch and hall, for example, which are considered to be the "mouth" of the home, it prevents sufficient chi from entering. If there is mess everywhere, chi will struggle sluggishly around the house.

Chi enters each room in the house and constantly forms spirals like wisps of smoke as it works its way from the door to the window. Chi also comes through the window and meanders toward the door.

This will in turn affect the occupants, making them feel confused or stuck in a rut. Feng shui consultants who are sensitive to energy flow may sense these stagnant areas by their stale, musty odor and a sticky feel.

THE ENERGY OF POSSESSIONS

When you surround yourself with articles that you love and often use, they emit a vibrant energy that encourages the normal flow of chi and helps to produce an atmosphere that makes your life feel joyful and happy. Loved possessions seem to support and nurture you through invisible connecting strands. However, if you surround yourself with unwanted junk or useless, broken items, their negative emanations will only pull you down. The longer these piles of trash stay around, the worse their effects. Throw away everything that has no particular meaning for you, and you will shed a heaviness and boost yourself mentally, physically, and spiritually.

When your home is a mess, it is difficult to find the things that you need. When your house keys have gone missing again, important letters have disappeared into the black hole that is a stack of junk mail, your cellphone has vanished, and those shoes you so want to wear are buried somewhere at the back of the closet—it's time for action. This constant muddle mixes up the energy from these items and you reflect this by becoming confused and stressed, rather than being calm and in command. So, by resolving the outer mess in your home and kick-starting the flow of chi, your inner confusion will disappear and life will certainly start to improve.

If your home is full of junk, you will constantly have problems finding items that you regularly use such as your keys, cellphone, and favorite pair of shoes.

Tied to your past

One of the problems that we all have with clearing out clutter is that we form such a strong emotional attachment to our possessions. Gazing fondly at ornaments or other accessories that people have given us over the years makes us feel secure. We even hang on to mementoes that are associated with an unhappy event, because we convince ourselves that we really do love them.

WHAT SHOULD YOU KEEP?

It is perfectly acceptable to keep some possessions that remind you of happy times, provided that when you look at them, you are filled with love. But if you have too many, your energies will be linked too strongly to your past, preventing new things from entering your life. Giving away or throwing out items that you strongly identify with can prove very painful emotionally, because it is like parting with a bit of yourself or rejecting a friend's generosity. When a friend selects a gift for you, it is chosen with a certain intention, often love, and these feelings then get tied up in the vibration of the object—which is why we find it so hard to let go of it. However, the truth is that once you have relinquished some possessions, you often don't miss them at all. Also, if you give them to someone who will love them just as much as you did, you will feel good about it.

DO YOU NEED TO PRUNE YOUR POSSESSIONS?

• Do your possessions mainly reflect your past?

• Look at your home objectively and see what it reveals—do you sense fear of the future in the chaos you have created?

• If you gave away several objects from your living room, would it really have a negative effect on your life?

• Are your deep feelings about some of your possessions holding you back from a brighter, better future?

• Do you see hosts of memories in all your rooms, and realize new ones are no longer being created?

If the answer to these questions is "yes," you definitely need to get rid of some stuff: so start pruning.

If you are finding it really hard to get rid of some items that you no longer use but which have wonderful memories, take photos of them and put them in bound books so when you throw them away you will not feel the loss so acutely.

RELEASING POSSESSIONS

It can be hard to give away or sell items inherited from deceased relatives. Even though you may never have liked a piece, it relates to that person in the form of an emotional tie, or energy, that you are reluctant to sever.

You may believe that your possessions are symbols of who you are. But when there are so many that they dominate your home, you may be subconsciously building a memorial to your past life—and if you let something go, it seems as if part of you is going as well. But once you have started this process of release, you will not look back and new energy will come flooding into your life.

Using the Pa Kua

If you are having a disastrous time in one area of your life and nothing seems to improve it, you should check to see if clutter is the cause of the problem. The Pa Kua is a basic feng shui tool. It is an octagonal figure that corresponds to the cardinal points of the compass as well as the four sub-directions. It contains eight ancient symbols called trigrams, which are believed to be very powerful. The Pa Kua has six rings. The first ring shows the trigrams; the second shows the Chinese name for the trigrams; the third ring relates to the five Chinese elements—Wood, Metal, and Earth have two directions, and Fire and Water have one. The fourth ring indicates the colors associated with each element; the fifth has the eight compass directions, while the sixth ring shows the life aspirations—the southeast, for example, corresponds to wealth and prosperity, while the north links to career prospects. The Pa Kua can be placed on a plan of the whole house, or a single room, to make a feng shui diagnosis. Various parts of the home represent each life aspiration, and these can be activated to improve your luck in that area.

HOW CLUTTER AFFECTS YOUR LIFE

Now go around your home to see how your clutter affects your life aspirations. If your largest pile of mess is in your wealth section, this explains why your finances have been suffering. If some is in your marriage area, it can bring problems to an existing relationship or prevent a new one; in your recognition and fame section, you can

Recognition and fame · South · Red · Fire · Li

Marriage and romantic happiness · Southwest · Yellow · Strong earth · K'un

Wealth and prosperity · Southeast · Green · Small wood · Sun

Children · West · Small metal · Metallic, white, gold · Tui

Family and health · East · Green, brown · Strong wood · Chen

Mentors and networking · Northwest · Metallic, white, gold · Strong metal · Ch'ien

Education and knowledge · Northeast · Beige · Small earth · Ken

Career prospects · North · Black, blue · Water · K'an

DRAWING A PLAN OF YOUR HOME

You need to find out where the eight life aspirations are in your home, so that you can see if they are being negatively affected by clutter.

- First, buy a good-quality orienteering compass. Then, with compass in hand, stand looking out of your front door to discover the direction that your home faces, making sure that you align the north end of the needle with the north point of the compass.

- Draw a scale plan of your home. Find the plan's center by drawing two diagonal lines from the corners and mark where they cross. Position the compass here.

- Mark the eight compass points on the plan: north, northeast, east, southeast, south, southwest, west, and northwest.

- Place a copy of the Pa Kua over the house plan, ensuring that the compass points match the Pa Kua sections. Note down which areas of your home relate to each life aspiration and then keep for reference.

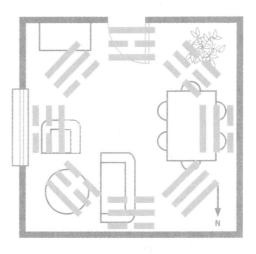

become less popular and lack enthusiasm. Clutter in your children's sector, for example, will inhibit your relationships with children and young people and hamper creativity; a blocked mentors and networking area shuts off support from friends and contacts, while a restricted career section will make your job seem like an endless struggle. Overflowing junk in your education sector limits your aptitude for learning and making good decisions. In your family area, clutter can cause regular conflict with family members.

Now that you know how the eight life aspiration areas of your home are afflicted, you can start by clearing out the worst area and see how fast changes can happen.

An orienteering compass is all that you need to get the basic directions of your home.

Clearing Out to Move On

There is no doubt about it—a cluttered home brings about a cluttered mind. If your household is bursting with vast amounts of clutter, chi stagnates and will not flow smoothly through each room. This can have a negative effect on you—you may feel that your life is in a rut, your confidence may plummet, or you may suffer from depression or tiredness. Holding on to possessions that you are emotionally attached to can keep you linked to the past and stop you moving forward in life.

To find out if you are hoarding unnecessary junk, fill in the questionnaire opposite. Take no more than five minutes to fill it in—your first answers are usually the most truthful. You can then start to work on the areas of your home that need the most attention.

Clearing out unwanted items from rooms such as the bathroom will help you to move on in your life.

ARE YOU A JUNK HOARDER?

This questionnaire will help you to assess just how much clutter has accumulated in your life. Score two points for a "Yes," one for a "Sometimes," and zero for a "No."

	Yes	No	Sometimes

1 Your closet is stuffed with clothes that you don't wear.

2 Odd socks and stockings that have seen better days lurk in bedroom drawers.

3 You keep magazines for more than a year.

4 You have several appliances that don't work, but never get around to getting them fixed.

5 Piles of newspapers are stacked for recycling, but you never take them to the recycling center.

6 Old sunscreen lotion bottles and discarded cosmetics hibernate at the back of the bathroom cabinet.

7 There is a cache of old sports gear or leisure equipment, which has been used once and then relegated to the attic, never to be seen again.

8 There is a drawer full of mysterious old keys that don't seem to open anything.

9 Piles of old, often not very good, vacation photos of people that you don't remember are now taking up cabinet space.

10 Your purse is awash with old notes, bus tickets, receipts from months ago, and other useless trivia.

11 Old files and papers and pens that don't work have found a permanent home in your briefcase.

12 Your car is rattling with apple cores and candy wrappers.

13 You are reluctant to invite friends to stay in your spare room because it has so much old furniture in it.

14 You have pieces of furniture that are all in need of some sort of repair.

15 Unfashionable and unloved ornaments are tucked out of sight in one of your drawers.

16 Your garage is so full of junk that you can't get the car in it anymore.

17 You have a collection of old, rusting garden equipment that you never use.

18 People keep tripping over all the boxes and other items that you store in the hall.

19 You still have theater or music concert programs from several years ago.

20 Your computer is crammed with files that you never refer to anymore.

TOTAL SCORE

THE RESULTS

15–20
Your home and life are well and truly cluttered. It's time to work out what you really want and what you can chuck out. Consider what storage you need for things you are keeping. Look at the storage you already have and decide how new furniture will fit in before buying any.

10–14
Clutter is building up, so get a grip on it now.

5–9
You do not have a problem with clutter yet, but do monitor yourself.

Below 5
Your home is clutter-free: try to keep it that way.

Space-clearing rituals

De-junking each room (see pages 34–81) helps stagnant chi flow freely again, but you may need a stronger method of changing the energy to suit different circumstances.

All the events that happen in a home create energies that become imprinted into its structure. Emotional upsets and illness leave a stronger impression, and patterns that repeat themselves get deeply imprinted. So if, for example, the previous occupants of your home got divorced, there is a likelihood that the people before them did as well, and that this powerful residual energy (predecessor energy) will cause relationship problems.

To shift and cleanse lurking negative energies, so that your life is not affected detrimentally, you need to perform a space-clearing ritual.

ENERGY BOOSTING TIPS

- Use these tips as additional ways of improving your home's energy.
- Give your home a good spring-clean to lift the energy.
- Bring more energy into the house by opening all doors and windows.
- Light candles to create yang, Fire energy.
- Arrange some fresh flowers, removing dried flowers or any dead or dying plants.

WHICH RITUAL DO I PERFORM?

There are some quite complicated rituals that require the services of an experienced space-clearing consultant, but you can do the following more simple techniques yourself.

Smudging: Smoldering herbal smudge sticks are a popular way of cleansing the energy of a home (see page 24).

Aromatherapy oils: A few drops of essential oil are added to a mister filled with water, and sprayed around to change the energy vibration (see page 26).

Clapping: This simple technique is used to shift energy that has become stuck in a room (see page 27).

Incense: The smoke from burning incense sticks is trailed around a room to change the energy levels (see page 28).

Natural salt: This traditional purification method helps neutralize negative energies.

HOW TO BEGIN

Do not attempt space-clearing if you are feeling physically or emotionally unwell, or if you are apprehensive about it for any reason. Avoid it if you are menstruating or pregnant, or have an open cut. Clean your home well the day before, have a bath or shower before you start, and take off any jewelry.

Candles can be used as basic energizers to lift the atmosphere in a specific room.

When to space-clear

If you want to generally clear the energies in your home, perform one of the space-clearing ceremonies detailed on the following pages. There are also particular times when creating an energy shift with these techniques will be beneficial to you and your family. Smudging and misting with essential oils are both very effective for deep cleansing. The other methods are best used in combination with these for intensive space-clearing.

AFTER AN ARGUMENT

The oppressive atmosphere that lingers after a serious argument hangs like a black cloud. It can be very unsettling and, if it is not dispelled, it can adversely affect the mood of people who enter the room. Misting with essential oils of lavender, chamomile, or geranium works well. To remove emotional negativity, just mist with water on its own. Water creates negative ions that flood the atmosphere, creating an invigorating feeling, similar to the euphoria felt by the sea. Incense, too, can shift heaviness.

Fresh-smelling herbs, such as sweetgrass, are used in dried form in the smudging technique to space-clear. Other herbs, such as basil, lemon, and lavender, are used in essential oil form and are diluted with water in a mister. The solution is sprayed around the home or room to clear the atmosphere. Lavender essential oil has the same effect as neutral chi and is therefore particularly effective for clearing bad, stuck energy.

AFTER ILLNESS OR DEATH

Wash the bed linen that was used in the sickroom, and do a space-clearing ceremony on the whole house so that you refresh all the energy. Thorough cleansing is advisable after death because although it is a natural process, grief and upset linger, and sometimes the person's spirit does not move on easily. Smudging with sweetgrass is powerful, and misting with essential oil of eucalyptus, lemon, tea tree, or rosemary lifts the atmosphere.

AFTER MOVING

History can repeat itself, so it is always a good idea to space-clear a new home, because there may be residual negative energies from previous owners. Smudging with sage or rosemary is beneficial, or you can mist with essential oil of lavender, sage, pine, fir, rosemary, or juniper. Use salt for extra cleansing power.

TO PROGRESS

Sometimes you are at a dead end in your life, perhaps unable to make any positive progress. Or there may be a problem that you can't resolve. But by space-clearing your home, you can change the energy of it and allow solutions to enter. Clapping shifts trapped energy, while misting with basil, lemon, and clary sage can improve mental clarity. Smudging with cedar needles is good for dispelling a dull atmosphere.

Herb plants can help to energize a room, while herb aromas have been used by native cultures to literally "clear the air."

Space-clearing techniques

SMUDGING

In ancient times, smoke was used in religious ceremonies for purification, and to make a connection with the spirits of the air. Smudging is a Native American tradition, often used by well-known space-clearer Denise Linn. Bundles of tightly-bound, dried herbs are lit and allowed to smolder. The stick is then carefully carried around a chosen area so that its smoke will cleanse any negative energies and purify the atmosphere.

A number of different herbs can be used for smudging ceremonies, but the most popular ones are sage, sweetgrass, rosemary, and cedar needles. Sage was popular traditionally for its strong purification powers, while sweetgrass, with a distinctive, fresh smell similar to new-mown hay, was believed to remove negative energies.

When you are smudging, make sure that you waft the smoke all around the room, including all the corners and nooks and crannies.

Buying herbs for smudging

Prepared herbal bundles for smudging, called smudge sticks, can be bought from natural health stores and some bookstores specializing in body, mind, and spirit titles. You can also make your own sticks by collecting herbs, tying the ends together with string, and hanging them upside-down in a cool place to dry.

The smudging ceremony

Light your smudge stick—you may need to blow on it to get it burning —and when it is well alight, extinguish the flames, leaving the herbs smoldering. Always hold the stick over a fireproof dish to catch any sparks. Before you begin to cleanse your home or a specific room, you should smudge yourself to clear your thoughts, emotions, and aura (your body's energy field). To do this, offer up your smoking herbs to the spirits, then, opening out your hands, draw the smoke gently toward your eyes and then the rest of your face and head. Slowly carry on drawing the smoke to the rest of your body and your aura, asking for cleansing of each area. This process will help to give you the energy to begin the purification of your home.

Smudging a room

Change into some casual or old clothes, wash your hands, and then, starting at the front door or the door of a specific room, walk clockwise around the room, holding the herbs and dish in one hand. With your free hand, waft the smoke along the walls and into all the corners, bookshelves, closets, and units. If the energy in one place feels heavier, waft the smoke into it more briskly. Ask the spirit of the property to

Sage and rosemary are two of the most popular herbs to use for space-clearing as they are good for removing any negative energies that may be present.

dispel negative energies and allow positive energy to flow once more. Smudging reaches deeply embedded old energy and releases it. As you finish, close the door.

Repeat the process in other rooms, if necessary. When you have finished the ritual, extinguish the stick under running water, cut off the burnt bit, and put away the stick (a small stick lasts for three smudging sessions; a large one for six or seven). Repeat the smudging technique every day, for two to three days, until the energy shifts, then smudge once a week as needed. Also, bear in mind that the smudging smoke is very pungent, so you will need to open windows and doors after each session to clear the atmosphere.

As you will have also cleansed your aura, your clothes and hair will smell of smoke, so you may need to wash your clothes and take a shower after the ceremony, and thoroughly wash your hair.

If you want to make your own smudge sticks, collect your chosen herbs, tie them with some string, and hang them upside down on a hook or nail to dry.

AROMATHERAPY

Essential oils are distilled naturally from herbs and plants. They have a wonderful smell and retain the life force, spirit, and energy of the plant from which they are extracted. They are normally extracted by steam distillation, which makes them around 70 percent stronger than the plants or herbs from which they are derived.

We all react to smell, and different essential oils can soothe, relax, or uplift us. Some also have strong cleansing properties, which can help to clear negative energies from the home.

Lavender is a good oil for general cleansing. It is believed to be the equivalent of neutral chi so can really help to shift stubborn energy, such as predecessor energy, which is imprinted on a building by previous occupants. Lime, orange, lemongrass, or peppermint oils are all good for stimulating the atmosphere. For general purification, the essential oils to use are juniper, sage, pine, or eucalyptus.

Finally, it is important that you like the aroma of the oils that you choose to mist with to energize the atmosphere. It is always a more effective and enjoyable exercise when you work with a scent that you really like.

Using the oils

Add a few drops of your chosen essential oil to a mister bottle filled with water and shake well. If you want to mist regularly, change the oil every couple of days, or keep the solution in a dark glass atomizer, as plastic can affect the oil's properties.

Stand still for a moment and close your eyes to set your intent for what you want the oils to achieve, and how you want the negative energies to be released. Then start at the door of the room to be cleansed and walk around it, spraying all around, paying particular attention to corners. Work your way through any other rooms that need cleansing. To bring about a dramatic change in energy, spray every day for a week, and then once a week as a top-up. If you're using lavender oil to deal with difficult predecessor energy, it is a good idea to spray every room every day for 28 days, as this represents a complete cycle of chi.

To give yourself a quick boost, fill a small glass atomizer with water and one or two drops of your favorite essential oil. Mist around your head and body to revitalize your skin and to cleanse your aura.

CLAPPING

This is a very simple, but effective, technique for dispersing energy blockages and making shifts in your life. Think of how clapping uplifts the atmosphere in a theater at the end of a performance.

Relax and set your intent for what you want to happen or change in your home. Stand with your feet slightly apart. Start in one corner: use small, quick claps to test the quality of the energy and larger, louder claps to shift energy. The claps should sound crisp and clear if the energy is good; if they are muffled or dull, it normally means that the energy is poor. To get rid of this dead energy, clap up and down in the corner, visualizing the energy clearing as you do it. Move on round the room, making small claps, until you get to another corner that needs clearing. You can also "clap out" closets, or work around electrical equipment to disperse the static electricity it generates.

Follow the same procedure in other rooms that need cleansing. When you have finished, rinse your hands under running water to remove any negative energy that may have clung to you. Repeat the clapping technique regularly to prevent any build-up of stale energy.

Clapping is a simple room cleansing technique, in which you clap all around the room to lift all the stale energy.

INCENSE

If you walk into churches or temples in different parts of the world, you will often notice the pleasant, smoky aroma of incense burning. Incense sticks are easy to use and quickly raise the vibrational level of the energies in a room. There are different types of incense available—choose carefully, since those made from synthetic substances may not have any effect on the energy in a room, or may even lower it. For powerful space-clearing, it is best to combine incense with another technique (see page 20).

The smell of incense also affects our senses. Hand-rolled varieties made from natural oils, gums, herbs, and spices and other ingredients work well.

Using incense

If you are combining the use of incense with another space-clearing method such as misting with essential oils, just light an incense stick, place it in a holder, and leave it smoldering in the background.

If you are using incense on its own, close your eyes, concentrating hard, and set your intent for that particular room or your home in general. Put the incense in a holder to carry around, light it, blow it out so that it starts smoking, and, starting at the door, slowly walk around the room wafting the smoke with your hand, concentrating on corners and dark areas. Repeat in other rooms, or set the incense on a side surface and leave it to burn out. Make sure it is positioned safely. Never leave burning materials unattended.

SALT

For centuries, salt has been used by different cultures to cleanse and purify negative energies, because of its ability to absorb impurities from the air. Salt is particularly good for enhancing other space-clearing techniques (see page 20) rather than just being used on its own. Rock or sea salt, kept in a sealed container, is best.

Salt for space-clearing

Sprinkle lines of salt across every doorway, place bowls of salt in corners and in the middle of rooms for deeper cleansing, or toss salt anywhere that you sense energy is stuck. Leave for 24 hours, then remove it or sweep it up. If the energies in a room seem to have come to a standstill, renew the salt bowls every day for about a week.

MAKING A HOME ALTAR

When you have cleansed the energies in your home, you may want to create a special place to use for quiet contemplation or meditation for a short time each day. Here you can put a small altar or shrine to help you get in touch with your spiritual side. Start by creating a focal point on the altar—this can be a representation of a religious deity, such as a Buddha, a photograph of a natural place that inspires you, or a picture of a person who helps you to connect spiritually. Include a favorite crystal and fresh flowers, and burn a candle or incense for a positive ambience whenever you use the altar. Set it up in a spare room or corner or place on a tray and store in a closet until needed.

Burning incense in a living room, for example, will bring in a wonderful aroma and dispel a bad atmosphere or any negativity after an argument.

Clutter Hotspots

The way your home looks reflects your personality. So, if it is disorganized and full of clutter, the way you run your life will be similar. If you have a family, you can't blame the disorder on them as they are also a reflection of you. Many of your rooms may be loaded with junk (see pages 34–81), but there are certain areas which, if they become crowded with clutter, can symbolically restrict you from enjoying life.

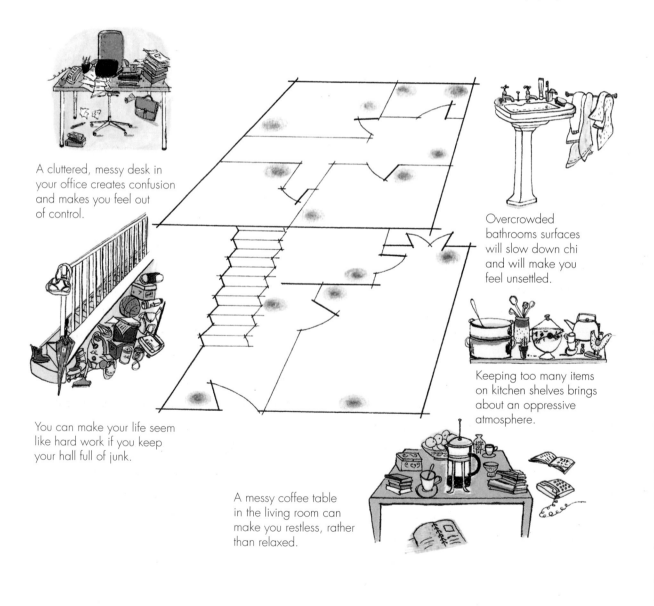

A cluttered, messy desk in your office creates confusion and makes you feel out of control.

Overcrowded bathrooms surfaces will slow down chi and will make you feel unsettled.

You can make your life seem like hard work if you keep your hall full of junk.

Keeping too many items on kitchen shelves brings about an oppressive atmosphere.

A messy coffee table in the living room can make you restless, rather than relaxed.

THE ENTRANCE AND HALL

This is considered to be the "mouth" of the home, where guests and friends enter and get their first impressions of where you live. It needs to be a bright, well-lit, welcoming environment that encourages chi to enter positively and meander through all the rooms in your home. All too often, this area is crowded with children's paraphernalia, shoes, bags, boxes, and newspapers, which make the energy slow and sluggish. If you have a pile of items stacked right by the entrance, it symbolizes life becoming a real struggle, with new opportunities barred.

ATTICS

These are the places where we tend to store our past. These areas are therefore often full of mementoes and memorabilia that simply restrain us so that we do not progress in life. By having a big clear-out, you will feel unburdened. Problems will no longer hang over you, and your aspirations for the future will no longer seem impossible.

BASEMENTS

Not everyone has a basement area, but if there is one in your house, the likelihood is that it is jammed full of unwanted or unused paraphernalia. This area symbolizes your past and is believed to be linked to your subconscious mind. If it is brimming with junk, then there may be things in your past that you have not addressed, or problems that you have been meaning to resolve for some time. It is really important to keep your basement orderly, because if it is neglected, it can have a detrimental effect on you, making you feel miserable, lethargic, and lacking a clear direction in life. If you often feel weighed down by the troubles of the world, it could be that all the clutter lurking in the basement is the cause of this feeling of immobility.

THE BACK DOOR

This is where everything leaves your home and is, therefore, a symbolic organ of excretion. So if the area is full of junk, the analogy is that your home will become constipated, so it is vital to keep it clear.

CORRIDORS AND PASSAGEWAYS

It is essential that chi flows easily through corridors to enable it to reach the upstairs or other parts of your home, so again any clutter will inhibit this process and should always be removed—common hotspots are either side of doorways and in wall recesses, so pay attention to these areas. If corridors and passageways are crowded, these energy conduits of the home will create feelings of restriction and an inability to progress in life.

The declutter plan

Before you start the plan, you need to assess what to keep or move, what to throw out, and what to give away. If you feel reluctant to do this, persevere, because clearing out rooms or spaces is therapeutic. It will release old energies and bring in fresh possibilities.

You may find that you have confused feelings about why you are so attached to certain objects that seem to have no further use in your life. Think about how you regard your space, consciously and subconsciously, and how you can avoid letting your rooms or possessions take control of you in future.

You do not have to throw everything out when you have your clear-out. In this bathroom, attractive storage baskets cleverly hold miscellaneous products.

ASSESSING YOUR JUNK

Now this is difficult. Go around your home and note down your main garbage areas, marking if they are large or small piles. Highlight the ones that irritate you the most, and start there first. Also pay attention to cluttered areas revealed by the Pa Kua (see page 16). If your career has been suffering and your career sector is full of trash, clear it out and see how your working life improves. Start slowly, tackling one closet or a room at a time, or the task will be too overwhelming.

BAG IT

Get five heavy-duty garbage bags, or some strong cardboard boxes. Label the first bag "junk" (all unwanted articles to go to the dump), the second bag "thrift store or friends" (useful items you've grown bored with, but which other people might like, or

It can be tempting to hide away unwanted goods or presents in suitcases, but this just brings about stagnancy in this area.

which could be sold), the third bag "things to be repaired or altered" (include items for renovation), and the fourth bag "things to sort and move" (useful articles that need a home). Fill a fifth bag with transitional items you can't quite let go of yet (keep for six months: if you miss them, they can be reinstated, if not, get rid of them).

With clothes, be tough: keep only those you enjoy wearing regularly—probably only a small percentage. Try on the ones you're not sure about, and if they don't fit or you dislike them, get rid of them. Make a conscious decision to never again purchase anything that you're not absolutely happy with.

JUNK CHECKLIST

It's categorized as junk if:

- it's broken and cannot be fixed;
- you dislike it every time you look at it;
- it was an unwanted present;
- it's an outmoded style or doesn't fit.

It's not junk if:

- you look at it with love and good feelings;
- it's something you really enjoy using;
- your work is helped by it.

Where the Spirit Rests

Abedroom is a personal haven, a place for letting go of the worries of the day. Here we want to feel nurtured, and be able to regenerate our mind, emotions, and spirit. It is a sanctuary for sleeping, reading, dreaming, making love, and sharing any secrets or upsets. The room therefore should be calm and tranquil.

The chi energy that flows through this area is very yin (passive) and will want to meander lazily. If your bedroom is crammed with too many items, the flow of chi will be hindered, denying you the relaxation and rejuvenation you seek. Clutter may also reveal the state

Wicker units blend with the calm of the bedroom. Keep fresh flowers out as they drain energy.

ENERGY GRIDLOCK

Chi moves into the messy bedroom and is held back from reaching the window by the crowded closet and the chair full of clothes. Chi entering by the window is slowed to the door by junk under the bed, the full dressing table, and an overcrowded bookcase.

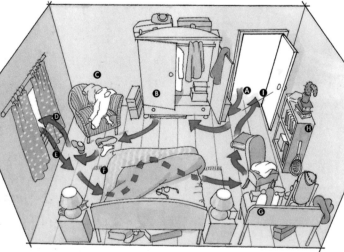

KEY:
A chi enters;
B overloaded closet;
C overladen chair;
D chi leaves;
E chi comes in window;

F clutter under bed;
G overstacked dressing table;
H full bookcase;
I chi leaves

ENERGY FREEWAY

Chi goes into the neat bedroom, traveling easily around the cleared closet and chair and out the window. Chi comes in the window and meanders through the empty under-bed space, over the clear dressing table, and then past the neat bookcase to leave the room.

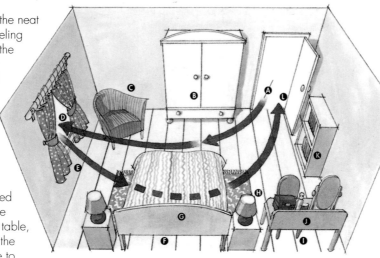

KEY:
A chi enters;
B clutter removed from closet;
C empty chair;
D chi leaves;
E chi comes in window;
F no clutter under bed;
G solid, supportive headboard;
H soft lighting from rounded lamps;
I natural wooden flooring;
J ordered dressing table;
K tidy bookcase with minimal books;
L chi leaves

of your love life. Is there a subconscious desire to keep a partner out of your life? Or does it reflect a chaotic marriage?

THE ENERGY TRAPS

Storing too much in the bedroom disturbs the harmonious flow of chi—so be firm with yourself.

Clothes: Are your closets and drawers bulging with clothes? Most of us wear only 20 percent of our wardrobes. If you can't throw clothes away, you can stay too attached to the past. Piles of discarded clothes create stagnant energy, so hang up your clothes each night and avoid sleeping with a laundry hamper in the bedroom—yesterday's attire gives off dead energy.

Under the bed: It is tempting to store things under the bed, but if you do, these items will create an energy blockage. Your bed should be a place that encourages good health and romantic happiness, but if there is heaviness underneath it, it can bring restless sleep and may disrupt your love life.

On top of bureaus: Suitcases, bedding, and boxes towering on bureaus will feel oppressive and affect your sleep, sometimes causing you to wake with a headache. Their looming presence may cause sluggishness and a reluctance to get up.

The dressing table: De-junk cosmetics clutter. Discard those extreme lip and nail colors—you won't fall in love with them one day—along with virtually empty lotion and fragrance bottles. Leave only fresh products that you use regularly.

A personal sanctuary

First, assess the room. Do you like its color and energy? Does it cosset you? Your bedroom should reflect your future dreams.

MAKING SPACE FOR LOVE

If you want a partner, are you really allowing room for one to enter? If your room contains mementoes from your last partner, you may also be subconsciously tying

A heaving closet full of too many unworn clothes can keep you too linked to your past. Dispense with what you don't need to make your "capsule wardrobe" which can be neatly stored away as above.

yourself to a past relationship. New lovers will absorb this energy and feel rejected by it. Also, sleeping in a bed that a long-term partner has slept in will still contain his or her energies, so either replace the bed or the mattress, or at least buy new bed linens. If you live with a partner, assess your space to see if the room reflects both of you; a troublesome relationship will normally be mirrored back at you. Remove, or at least cover at night, televisions, computers, and mirrored closet doors, as they are too yang. If you're happy on your own, appraise your room to see if it is a sensuous niche. Does its contents show where you are at, or where you want to be?

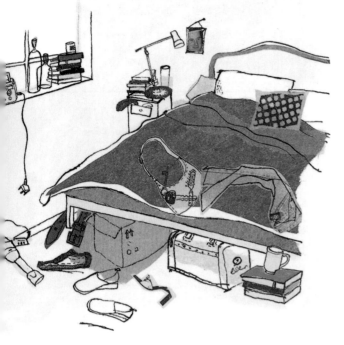

COLOR, MOOD, AND LIGHTING

The vibrational energy that comes from your bedroom colors has a profound affect on you. Good feng shui colors are shades of red—orange, soft pinks, and apricot shades promote sensuality. Pastel blues, greens, and lavender are calming and create a feeling of serenity.

Consider lighting carefully. Dimmer switches create a softer mood, while bedside lamps with rounded shades give a warm glow for night reading. Flickering candles add romance; incense and the scent of geranium from an aromatherapy burner create fragrant relaxation. Put out candles before sleeping.

Junk that is thrown under the bed becomes stuck energy and can affect your health (top left). Clear out unnecessary goods and store your essentials in this blanket box (left). Place moveable items on top so that you can have easy access to its contents. Natural wood flooring encourages a good flow of chi.

Ordered bliss

Now you have appraised your bedroom possessions, you need to look at storage solutions to hide them all away and create the peaceful atmosphere that is so needed

By planning in adequate shelving units that will hold a variety of clothing, you can make your bedroom a serene and well-ordered environment.

here. Are there any alcoves where you could fit an extra unit? Remember your overall goal is clean, ordered surfaces and tidy chests and cabinets, so that the chi entering the bedroom flows smoothly.

STORAGE SOLUTIONS

Clothes and shoes: Look at what you have left: is it really now a "capsule" closet of

BEDROOM CLUTTER CHECKLIST

If your room is a clutter nightmare, search through everything and make your five distinct piles (see page 33).

- Clothes and shoes: empty your closets and drawers, rationalizing what you really love to wear—and what you don't.
- Jewelry: remove broken items and pieces hardly worn.
- Cosmetics, lotions, perfumes, and aftershaves: are these congealed or virtually finished?
- Bedding: is this piled on top of the closet? Store elsewhere, and throw out old or torn linen.
- Books and magazines: be ruthless and keep to a minimum. Too many books in the bedroom is not good feng shui.
- Boxes of old sports gear, broken appliances and general clutter: if scattered around the room and under the bed, throw out now, or store properly elsewhere.

your favorite items? Separate summer and winter clothes, and store those that are not currently used in a closet or suitcase in the spare room. If you have only one bedroom, see if you are making best use of the available space— tall, wicker or rattan-style units with several shelves come in different sizes and fit well in recessed corners. They can easily swallow up a pile of sweaters, tops, shirts, T-shirts, and shorts.

How about increasing your closet's efficiency by fitting tiered racks for your shoes, or maybe adding canvas or mesh hanging racks for sweaters and skirts? If your closet has shelves, slot in different-sized clear plastic boxes for view-at-a-glance storage. Multiple hangers also help maximize hanging space.

Store socks, stockings, underwear, and ties in boxes that fit neatly into drawers or partitioned boxes on shelves.

Linen and bedding: These can be hidden in blanket boxes or wicker baskets at the foot of the bed.

Cosmetics and jewelry: Tidy current cosmetics into neat, clear plastic boxes with compartments that enable tubes or brushes to stand upright. A set of small woven baskets would also work well. Sort jewelry into tiered boxes.

Books and magazines: Keep only one or two current magazines here and minimal books. Place favorite books on a small bookshelf or in a bedside cabinet.

Miscellaneous items: Don't store them in a drawer unit under the bed; keep elsewhere or in a stacking unit in the closet.

Handy plastic boxes can be slipped into narrow drawers to hold socks, underwear, or scarves.

Peace and Stimulation

Your children's bedroom is their own special place. As well as being somewhere to sleep, it is their refuge from the world, where they can play games, read, give rein to their creative abilities, settle down to their homework, hang their favorite posters, entertain friends, and listen to music.

Although primarily for rest, the room is also an area where children need stimulation for homework and hobbies, so it benefits from positive chi energy. If their bedroom is overcrowded with unloved toys, sports gear, or school items, the flow of chi will be hampered and this will make children unable to think clearly or to act in a positive way.

THE ENERGY TRAPS

Children are notoriously messy, often leaving toys and books strewn across the floor. But this trail of chaos disrupts the atmosphere and can disturb their sleep, so cajole them to tidy up on a regular basis.

Play or work areas: If these are an explosion of cars, dolls, games, CDs, computer games, and schoolwork, it will distort chi and prevent children getting good-quality sleep.

Overloaded closets: If the doors will not shut because of all the goods stacked inside, a feeling of oppression will permeate the room (see page 22). Children may also subliminally worry that everything

ENERGY GRIDLOCK

Chi moves into the children's messy bedroom and is stopped by an overladen closet. Its route to the window is further hampered by clothes and toys on the floor and clutter under the beds. Chi entering through the window is restricted on its way to the door by a crowded play table and books and clothes strewn on the floor.

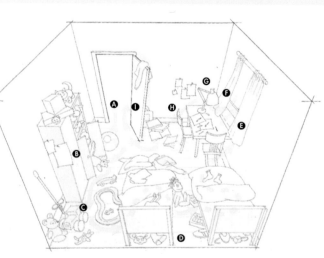

KEY:
A chi enters;
B bulging closet;
C scattered clothes and toys;
D clothes and toys under beds;
E chi leaves;
F chi flows in window;
G jumbled play table;
H books and toys piled on floor;
I chi leaves

Small hanging units add to the look of the bedroom and provide a place to display small painted toys.

ENERGY FREEWAY

Chi weaves into an ordered bedroom and flows evenly around a cleared-out closet and stored toys, and through empty under-bed space to the window. Chi proceeds through the window and slides over an ordered play table and around the bare floor to the door.

KEY: **A** chi enters; **B** re-planned closet; **C** bag for dirty clothes; **D** toys stored in stacking boxes; **E** no mess under beds; **F** rounded bedside lamps; **G** fabric wallhanging to slow chi; **H** chi leaves; **I** chi comes in window; **J** structured play table; **K** desk lamp for schoolwork; **L** cleared floor; **M** chi leaves

will fall on top of them—despite the fact that they created the situation in the first place.

Clothes: Although children don't hang on to clothes because they are emotionally attached to them, they are adept at leaving them in scattered heaps, sources of stale energy that make the bedroom's atmosphere sluggish and dull.

Under the bed: As with an adult's bedroom (see page 33), keep this area clear.

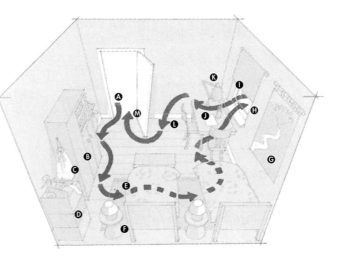

Keeping the children's bedroom tidy is a constant battle, so have plenty of tiered storage and make it a rule that all toys need to be put away at night.

A magical hideaway

Clearing up your children's bedroom will make you and them feel better (see checklist) —despite what they might say! But before you do this, pause and study the room. Appraise the furniture, the paint color or wallpaper, the posters, and pictures. Do they reflect your children as they are today, or is the room linked to the past? Have they been sleeping well, or possibly complaining of disturbed nights? Like an adult's bedroom, the children's room needs to be comfortable and somewhere that nurtures their developing personality and spirit.

THE RIGHT ATMOSPHERE

If the room looks chaotic, your children's behavior and schoolwork may mirror this, with difficulty in focusing on projects, and failure to achieve the grades of which they

Toys that are left scattered around the bedroom will make your children feel unsettled and restless. Tidy soft toys away in hanging storage bags or handy soft baskets, such as these (above).

CHILDREN'S BEDROOM CLUTTER CHECKLIST

- Go through the room with your children, sorting out their toys and other equipment according to the five-bag system (see page 33).
- Toys: throw away broken items and give away any that are unwanted.
- Books: reserve the favorites and give away old titles to deserving recipients such as hospitals.
- Computer games: see if you can sell or exchange the ones that have fallen from favor.
- Clothes: rationalize the clothes that are actually worn and pass on ones that are too small to younger children.

are capable. The room's energy will also seem heavy, making them listless and lacking in enthusiasm.

If your children are sleeping in bunk beds, move them to separate beds as soon as you can, as the child on the bottom can feel restricted or compressed. In a teenager's room, a computer should be screened off so that its yang energies don't affect sleep. Avoid having a television in the bedroom, but if there is one, make sure it does not face the bed, and unplug it at night to reduce electromagnetic stress.

COLOR, MOOD, AND LIGHTING

Most children react strongly to color. Bright colors and busy wallpaper designs can look good, but may be too stimulating for very active children; soft pastel colors, purples, blues, and greens

A chaotic bedroom (left) can give children problems with sleeping. Storage in primary colors (above) is appealing and works well with children who are not too active. Pull-down blinds conceal larger toys.

will calm them. Give quieter children a boost with pinks or oranges, and encourage creative children to thrive with shades of yellow.

Bedroom lighting is normally soft and ambient, but because of the mixed activities in children's rooms, good task lighting is important. Place a desk lamp in the study area, and a sufficiently bright bedside lamp for reading as young eyes can strain easily.

Fabric or paper mobiles hung near the cot or bed, but not over it, are very relaxing for babies and toddlers. Restrict teenagers from having a vast collection of action-packed or violent posters, as they are too stimulating.

Stored benefits

Once you and your children have battled over their possessions, glance around their bedroom and see where you can create more storage. Don't forget that hanging units take up very little space. As this is a multiactivity room, for sleep and play, you need to leave clear floor space so that positive chi can move freely through it.

Ingenious canvas hanging racks with numerous pockets can hold tiny toys and small pieces of clothing.

Painting a storage unit in a bright color with a stenciled pattern can make it blend into the background.

STORAGE SOLUTIONS

Toys and games: Children always have their favorites, so make sure that these are readily available. Try to get children to tidy up every night, explaining that they will feel better if they do so. Wooden chests or blanket-style boxes will hold soft toys. Transparent or colorful plastic stacking boxes, which can stand on the floor or sit in a wooden unit, are great for building blocks and small plastic toys. Fabric-covered boxes with lids are also useful and will stack on top of each other. For toy soldiers and other very small items, wooden units with several shallow drawers are ideal. Canvas or cotton hanging sacks, suspended from

hooks on the wall or closets, will hold miscellaneous items. Games, which are more bulky, are best stacked on to wooden or metal shelf units.

Books: Keeping too many books in the bedroom can be over-stimulating, so try to persuade your children to retain only a select few here, stowed neatly on bookshelves.

Computer games, disks, and CDs: This form of clutter is particularly prevalent in teenagers' rooms. It is hard to get teenagers to be tidy, but persuade them to stash disks and CDs in plastic boxes or on bookshelves, and put software disks and computer-related manuals out of sight in closets or on shelves.

Clothes and shoes: Brightly patterned cotton hanging units hold several pairs of young children's shoes. For older children and teenagers, tiered shoe racks or hanging canvas or mesh racks fit inside closets (see page 39). If you are replanning the room, think about installing fitted closets with good hanging space and several shelves so that sweatshirts, T-shirts, and other items can be piled here, perhaps within pull-out plastic boxes. Again, make the most of hanging space with multiple hangers (see page 39).

Discourage children from leaving clothes on the floor at night. Clothes should be hung up, or placed in a canvas sack or in a laundry hamper.

Bright plastic storage boxes on wheels hold a lot and can be easily moved around the bedroom. Do not store them under the bed regularly, as this can cause disturbed sleep.

A Nurturing Place

Often considered the "heart" of the home, the kitchen is where the family gather to eat, chat, and relax. It should be a warm, cozy environment, where everyone feels cocooned by its comforting ambience, and where senses are stimulated by wonderful cooking smells.

The kitchen has become a room of many other functions too: children do their homework, adults steal half an hour to read a newspaper or book, and friends drop in for a chat and a coffee. And because this is the room where the family is fed and nurtured, the energy that moves through it needs to be positive and very yang. Cluttered counters, refrigerators, cabinets, and floors will block chi flow, preventing the balance and harmony that is required.

THE ENERGY TRAPS

If you can never find that spice jar or bag of flour that you want because your cabinets are overstocked, or if you are constantly searching for the right kitchen accessory on your crowded counters, a good clear-out is well overdue.

Good feelings of warmth and contentment should abound in a kitchen area. Keeping surfaces clear and having enough shelving and kitchen units will promote a good flow of energy.

ENERGY GRIDLOCK

Chi comes into a crowded kitchen and its progress toward the window is hindered by too much stored on cabinets, a full trash can, and full sink. The smooth movement of chi through the window to the door is stopped by crowded shelves and a messy floor.

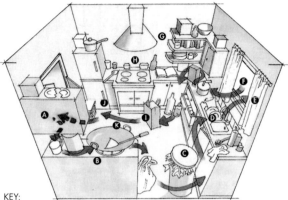

KEY:

A chi enters; B overstacked cabinets; C overflowing trash can; D cluttered sink; E chi leaves; F chi comes in window; G overladen shelves; H crowded counters; I littered floor; J newspapers; K chi leaves

Cabinets and kitchen units: Overloading these will create a very oppressive atmosphere. Check use-by dates of packaged goods—if they have expired, you are allowing negative energies to enter this area. Stale energy is also created by unwanted or cracked utensils.

Work surfaces: If you fill your counter tops with too many utensils, gadgets, storage jars, and other kitchen items, chi will be slowed down and this can adversely affect how you feel when cooking and eating in the kitchen.

Trash cans: An overflowing trash can creates negative energy and will seriously block energy flow, so empty it regularly.

ENERGY FREEWAY

Chi flows easily into a tidy kitchen, around cleared rubbish, over a clean sink, and out of the window. Chi comes in the window and can freely move over neat shelves, around an ordered trash can and tidied floor, and out of the door.

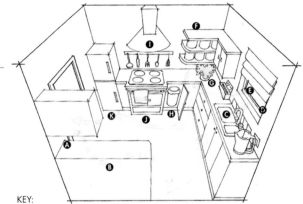

KEY:

A chi enters; B cleared cabinets; C empty sink; D chi leaves room; E chi comes in window; F structured shelves; G energizing plant; H empty, hidden trash can; I hanging utensils; J empty floor; K chi leaves

Refrigerators and freezers: These should always be full of food to symbolize the family's good health and wealth, but again, keep an eye on use-by dates, because storing expired goods could be very detrimental to the family's welfare.

Appliances: Positive energy is given off by electrical equipment in the kitchen, but if broken appliances are left to fester on counters, they will bring about energy blockages that will affect the room's happy atmosphere.

The floor area: Bottles, newspapers, and other items stacked haphazardly on the kitchen floor will look untidy and also make the flow of chi very sluggish.

A place of nourishment

Removing food that is no longer fresh from the kitchen and getting appliances mended will make you feel better (see checklist), but you'll need to tune into the atmosphere, too. Do you like the room, and does its energy embrace you? Or do you feel irritated because counters are cluttered and the cabinets are a mess?

   If your cabinets contain enough packaged goods to keep you going for years, then you are missing out on the nurturing environment your family needs. Why are you hoarding so much food—are you subconsciously worried that you will not have enough? Does it stem from a childhood where food was restricted? Try to keep a more sensible stockpile.

Crowding too much kitchenware on open shelves (above) creates distraction and disturbance, so clear out what's not needed and display attractive glasses, tableware, and storage jars (left).

INSPECT THE STOVE

If the burners are clogged, you will restrict positive Fire energy, reduce the benefit you get from your food, and maybe inhibit your wealth potential. If the stove is positioned right next to the sink or refrigerator/freezer, this produces a conflict between Fire and Water, which will disrupt the atmosphere of the room. Avoid this by placing a wood or metal unit between them to create a barrier. If your kitchen table is under a beam, it will be affected by downward "cutting" chi, which is bad feng shui. Cutting chi will also affect tables that are close to sharp corners, which can prove harmful. Both can cause conflict at mealtimes, so move the table away from the beam and block cutting chi with plants.

COLOR, MOOD, AND LIGHTING

A kitchen needs to be airy and inviting, so white works well here—to the Chinese, this symbolizes purity. The ideal kitchen location is in the east or southeast sector of the house (Wood), so if yours faces in this direction you can enhance it with shades of green (Wood) or blue (Water), because according to the relationship between the five elements, which operate in a cycle, Water produces Wood. Wooden flooring and units add natural warmth.

Be careful not to use a strong red in a south-facing (Fire) kitchen, because it will emphasize the element too strongly, although white and metal accessories can counter this.

Good lighting brings in positive yang energy, so add downlighters or spotlights, and use strip lighting under units to illuminate food preparation areas.

Messy sinks, overflowing trash cans, and other garbage all upset the harmony in the kitchen (above). Concealing the trash can in a unit and storing other kitchen goods away neatly will make the room seem calm but inviting. White is a good kitchen color as it symbolizes purity (left).

Streamlined stocks

If you're suffering from exhaustion, having ruthlessly battled through the kitchen evaluating what you really do and do not need, take a short break to think about how you can increase your storage options for all the items that are left. See if you have space for more cabinets, shelves, or wall units.

STORAGE SOLUTIONS

Packaged goods, sauces, and canned food: If you have a fitted kitchen and packaged goods are still too numerous to store in the units, consider adding extra units. Slimline cabinets will take advantage of a small gap.

Dishes and glasses: Make a feature of these by displaying them in an open-fronted unit in a kitchen or dining area. Pine dressers and wooden or painted units with glass doors also do the job.

Fruit and vegetables: A good way of storing these quickly consumed foods is to pack them in plastic baskets, and push these into either an open-fronted or closed unit under the counter. Wicker baskets also look good when used individually or stacked together and slid under counters. When space is tight, fresh produce can be placed in metal mesh baskets hung from a hook in the wall or the ceiling. Alternatively, a chrome cart with basket shelves is useful because it can be quickly wheeled out of sight.

Cleaning goods: All too often these disappear into a dark jungle under the sink, and it's difficult to identify what's living there. One solution is to fit a wire container with different compartments that slides in and out on runners. Or separate the items into different baskets or plastic boxes and stack on the shelves of the sink unit.

Utensils and gadgets: On kitchen counters, keep these to a minimum. House sharp knives in cutlery units or wooden knife blocks. Never hang knives on a magnetic rack, because the sharp points will create harmful cutting chi. Other utensils can be suspended from hooks on a rail, possibly positioned above the stove. Pans or cups can also be hung from rails if you have limited unit space.

Miscellaneous items: A kitchen cart is a useful object and can sit under a counter or at the side of the kitchen when not in use. Its tiled or wooden top gives you an extra preparation surface, while bottles of wine or regularly used dishes, utensils, or drying cloths can be stored on the bottom. Many contain drawers or handy hanging rails.

Storage jars, preserves, and pasta jars: These are good candidates for display, so clear them from counter tops and place on simple open shelving. You can put up narrow shelves or racks to hold all your spices, making them easily accessible, and liberating some space in your cabinets.

Appliances: Only leave out the ones that you use regularly, such as the toaster, the electric kettle, and coffee machine. Store other items such as the iron, liquidizer, juicer, and food processor in deep drawer units, or in cabinets with deep shelves.

KITCHEN CLUTTER CHECKLIST

- Go through all your cabinets, sorting out items according to the five-bag system (see page 33).
- Packaged goods, sauces, and cans of food: check for stale goods and those past their use-by date and throw out.
- Bottles, newspapers, old cartons, and carrier bags: recycle these items, and take to the recycling center regularly. Keep carrier bags for re-use.
- Appliances: if an appliance is broken, get it fixed or dispense with it.
- Trash cans: try to empty daily as they breed stagnancy in an otherwise positive area.
- Under the sink: sort through cleaning products and materials and only keep those you use regularly—get rid of impulse buys that have never been used.
- Refrigerator and freezer: check each shelf, removing items that aren't fresh and out-of-date products.
- Work surfaces: minimize utensils and recycle glass storage jars.

When you have thrown out the kitchen goods that are not needed, display pleasing products such as storage jars and vinegars and oils on open shelving.

The "Mouth" of the Home

The front entrance and hall of your home are the first places friends and visitors see when they call around. It reflects your personality—a place of joyous welcomes and sad farewells. From here you view the world from both the inside and outside. The hall should be bright and welcoming—an area that invites people in.

Chi, the beneficial energy that creates balance and harmony, enters through the front door—the "mouth" of the home—fulfiling the same function as food entering our bodies. Chi needs to flow in strongly and positively without obstruction, so cut back any overgrown plants or trees around the doorway, because they will inhibit its movement. If, once it enters the home, it has to struggle around items such as boxes, baby strollers, and an overflowing coat rack, the symbolic meaning of this is that you are finding life hard work.

ENERGY GRIDLOCK

Chi comes through the front door, is obstructed by objects behind the door, and is prevented from moving up the stairs by blockages. Chi going down the hall is restricted by too many items and a bulging closet.

KEY:
A chi enters;
B boxes and shopping trolley;
C notes on mirror;
D chi goes up stairs;
E obstacles on stairs;
F chi goes down hall;
G overladen coat rack;
H bike and other clutter;
I closet full of junk;
J chi leaves

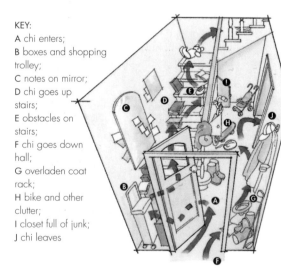

ENERGY FREEWAY

Chi meanders into an ordered home, is slowed by the wind chime, and moves effortlessly around a storage unit and clean mirror and up well-lit, cleared stairs. Chi going down the hall flows around a neat coat rack and umbrella stand, along the empty floor, and past a plant which slows chi, and an ordered closet.

KEY:
A chi enters;
B put wind chime over door;
C storage unit and key holder;
D mirror;
E well-lit, inspirational pictures;
F cleared stairs;
G chi goes down hall;
H organized coat rack;
I healthy plant;
J empty floor;
K rationalized closet;
L chi leaves

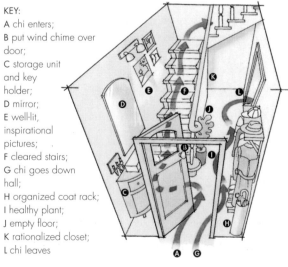

The hall is the first place that visitors see when they enter your home, so it needs to be uncluttered with a bright and inviting atmosphere and good lighting.

THE ENERGY TRAPS

An overcrowded hall, where everybody sees fit to leave miscellaneous items scattered haphazardly all over the floor, will soon start to wear you down. You may feel your life is losing direction, and because chi can't enter this area properly, you will be restricted in everything you are trying to do, and new opportunities will be blocked.

The porch and hall: Tripping over old umbrellas, golf clubs, bikes, baby strollers, boxes, muddy shoes or boots will cause constant annoyance and irritation. The hampered flow of chi will disturb the atmosphere, making visitors uneasy as they enter your home.

Hall table or desk: Stacks of local newspapers, junk mail, and unpaid bills are stale energy and will slow down your progress in life.

Alcoves: These are dangerously shaped for attracting clutter and so forming negative energies—so beware!

Stairs: If you leave files, books, and papers on the stairs, you will restrict the energy flow through the home and feel a heaviness every time you go upstairs.

Under the stairs: If this is your "black hole" where every possible items of junk and home repair items gravitate toward, their stale energy will seep out into other areas of your home. This can make the people who live there feel lethargic and depressed.

HALL CLUTTER CHECKLIST

Rationalize what to keep and what to throw away, making piles to put into your five-bag system (see page 33).

- Shoes, boots, walking shoes, sports shoes: return them to the closet, or to the garbage if they are worn out.

- Junk mail, newspapers, bills, keys: sort through the piles, then file the essentials and recycle or dispense with the rest.

- Coat rack: check through all the jackets and coats, decide what is currently used and throw away or store the remainder elsewhere.

- Bikes, baby strollers, golf clubs, sports gear: if these are now redundant, sell or give away; alternatively, find good storage solutions.

- Home repair goods: get rid of dried-up paints, old glues, or other out-of-date products that may be lurking under the stairs.

The inner world

Removing obstructions from your hall and entrance will help you to move on in life (see checklist), but also study its overall atmosphere. Is it bright and inviting, or dark and restricting? Does it echo how you feel about your life?

HALL LAYOUT PROBLEMS

If your entrance and hall are a mess, ask yourself why you are stopping good things coming into your life. See how your door opens—does it get blocked by clutter inhibiting the chi? Look at the geography of the area. According to feng shui, a staircase should not start directly opposite the main door, and a curved staircase is preferable to one that is straight. If your stairs do face the door, hanging wind chimes over the front door will help slow down the flow of energy.

COLOR, MOOD, AND LIGHTING

A warm, welcoming light outside and good ceiling lighting inside will encourage people in. To expand a narrow hall, hang a mirror on a side wall. To lead people to the first floor, put up well-lit inspirational pictures along the stairs. As this area needs to be welcoming, soft pastel blues, greens, pinks, or shades of white or cream are soothing colors for walls and paintwork.

Opposite: Shades of white or soft pastels can help to expand a narrow hall. This area need not be stark; when you have removed any clutter, hang inspiring pictures, fit interesting lights, and add chairs, tables, or small storage units.

Left: Too many coats, jackets, and scarves can overwhelm coat racks, so give away those you don't need and choose a functional style that works for you and your family.

STORAGE SOLUTIONS

After your major clear-out, muse about new storage solutions that will blend with the pleasant ambience of this area. An interesting oriental pot can hold umbrellas.

Shoes, boots, and sports shoes: A tiered plastic or metal shoe rack in the porch or by the front door will hold several pairs of shoes. Or install neat wooden cabinets with hinged drawers, or a tall, slim cabinet that combines sloping shelves for shoes at the bottom with other useful shelves above.

Hats, coats, and jackets: Choose a coat rack with rails for hanging items, and a flat area on top for hats and scarves. Or, place a conventional coat stand in an unused corner. There are also slimline units with outer hooks and sliding doors concealing shoe shelves.

Junk mail, bills, and keys: A desk or low wooden storage unit with drawers can house these items. Hang keys on the wall behind for easy access. Clip interesting flyers together and file in drawers or cardboard files. Put bills in a plastic folder with compartments.

Bikes, strollers, sports gear, and home repair items: Preferably, store bikes in a garage or shed, or under the stairs. Suspend a stroller from a strong hook under the stairs or in a hall closet; likewise hang golf clubs and sports gear. There are special under-the-stair units for open staircases, with different sized plastic stacking units. These are ideal for home repair paraphernalia.

Sociability and Relxation

The living room is the focal point of the home, where the family gathers to unwind from the relentless pressures of daily life. It is where lively conversations about the state of the country or the meaning of life can stretch long into the night. It is a special meeting place, where old and new guests are welcomed and entertained.

The living room is often multifunctional, with one area for relaxing, another for dining, and a corner for a home office, from which the household is run and organized.

Although this is essentially a tranquil room, the living room is also a sociable place and

A well-planned seating layout in your living room adds to its appeal and conviviality. Making sure it is junk-free will aid energy movement and sociability.

needs a positive chi movement in order to keep conversations flowing and to create a good, uplifting ambience. If the room is cluttered or over-furnished, the energy will

ENERGY GRIDLOCK

Chi streams into the crowded living room and on its way to the window, hits DVDs on the floor and struggles around a piled bookcase and coffee table. It is slowed by clutter behind the sofa, boxes of wine, and a muddled cabinet. From the window to its exit through the door, it is restricted by the crowded table, furniture, and floor.

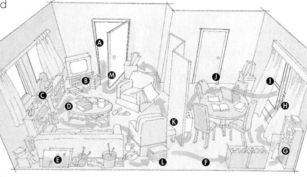

KEY:
A chi enters;
B piles of DVDs;
C overstacked bookcase;
D messy coffee table;
E piles of junk and CDs;
F unwanted boxes;
G too full unit;
H chi leaves;
I chi comes in window;
J untidy table;
K jumbled floor;
L mess behind furniture;
M chi leaves

stagnate, engendering unsettled and restless feelings, rather than the desired feeling of contentment and relaxation.

THE ENERGY TRAPS

Finding a big piece of furniture barring your way when you enter your living room, or having to navigate round piles of newspapers, magazines, and other paraphernalia, is at odds with the aim of creating a relaxing, sociable atmosphere, so you need to do some clearing and streamlining.

Behind sofas: Your sofa can be a clutter magnet. If the area behind your sofa conceals a morass of discarded craft projects, unhung pictures, leaflets, and packets of old photographs, you have created a brooding stagnancy behind you that will disturb you every time you sit down.

On bookshelves: Symbolically, books are linked to your likes and beliefs, so if there are a lot of dusty old books sitting on the shelves, it indicates that you are becoming very set in your ways.

Overcrowded mantles: A vast assortment of ornaments, candlesticks, dishes, and ashtrays looks unsightly and will induce a restless energy.

Under coffee tables: Overflowing piles of magazines will bring about a central area

ENERGY FREEWAY

Chi enters the well-planned lounge, sweeping around the revamped TV storage unit, bookcase and plant, around the empty coffee table and tidied floor, to the cleared unit and out of the window. The chi that enters by the window streams over the polished table, over the clean floor, and out the door.

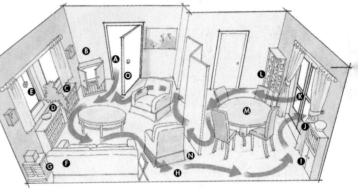

KEY:
A chi enters;
B stacked TV unit;
C tidy bookcase;
D energizing plant;
E hanging crystal to slow energy;
F cleared furniture;
G CD unit;
H bare floor;
I organized unit;
J chi leaves;
K chi enters;
L extra storage unit;
M empty table;
N cleared floor;
O chi leaves

of stale energy that will slow down all of the family.

Overstocked cabinets or units: Stacks of old DVDs, CDs, and other items, piled haphazardly on top of each other, link you too much to your past, rather than your future. Chi will be very sluggish here, and actually make people reluctant to play music at all.

Bar: If, when you open the door, the first thing that you see is odd, cracked glasses and almost empty bottles of spirits, the mess and disorder will bring you down.

The comfort zone

Getting down to the task of refining your main living space and making it more homely is very rewarding, but before you start your clear-out (see checklist), take time to assess this area where you spend so much of your time, to see what it says about you. Does its decor and furnishings welcome you, or are they looking tired and shabby, maybe reflecting what you are secretly feeling about life? Are you keeping it cluttered and overcrowded as a symbol of your refusal to let changes happen in your life?

ROOM TO RELAX?

A cluttered living room will deter guests from lingering. If your room is like this, it may reveal a subconscious desire to keep people away.

Pay attention to the positioning of furniture: sofas and chairs are best placed in a semi-circle around a coffee table or in front of the fire so that they face each other, making it

It is hard to relax in a room which is full of unloved and discarded items (left). Keep as little as possible on coffee tables (above) and display your favorite, loved possessions on attractive storage units.

Regularly go through your books and review what you really need as too many old ones can make you set in your ways (left). Place your favorite books and treasured artefacts that are left on well-lit shelving.

easy for people to chat. Never put chairs under a beam, because the cutting chi that comes down from it can cause headaches. Sharp edges and pointed structures channel bad feng shui, referred to as poison arrows. To avoid your suffering from the effects of these, furniture such as shelves with sharp edges can be obscured with trailing plants, while sharp-angled tables can be covered with cloth made from interesting fabrics. In a large living area, a dining area can be demarcated with shelving units or large sofas.

COLOR, MOOD, AND LIGHTING

Shades of cream or soft pastel colors create a relaxing ambience. Yellow will expand a room and helps to stimulate conversation. Alternatively, you could paint the room in

relation to the room's element according to the Pa Kua. So if it faces north, for example, it should be blue, but if it faces south a shade of red is appropriate (see page 16).

Lighting is important in a living room to draw in good yang energy. Use uplighters or pendant lights for background lighting, lamps for mood lighting, and spotlights for accent lighting on pictures, ornaments, and plants. The soft, natural light of candles adds a special appeal. To promote a feeling of calm, wellbeing, and harmony, burn fragrant incense or essential oils.

Structured tranquility

Clearing out items from this room is never easy, but you will immediately notice an uplift in its energy when you do so. Walk around the room and decide how you can improve the storage of your remaining possessions. If you adore books and still have many left, appraise where you might fit in another shelving unit.

STORAGE SOLUTIONS

Books: Consider building shelves into any unused alcoves—you can also put a cabinet underneath the shelves that will hold other miscellaneous goods. A wide, freestanding open wooden bookcase will hold many titles. Try to intersperse sections of books with ornaments to break up the solidity of its appearance. Buy a bookcase on rollers so that it can be moved around easily, or used as a room divider for separating the dining and relaxation areas.

Photographs: Go through these carefully, only keeping those that fill you with love

Take your CDs off the floor and house them in stylish wooden cabinets such as this one.

LIVING ROOM CLUTTER CHECKLIST

Work methodically through your living room items, making distinct piles to put into your five-bag system (see page 33).

- Books: be ruthless—keep the special ones, but sell the rest or give to thrift stores or a hospital.
- Wallets of photographs: these create dull energy, so sort through them all and put the pictures that give you joy into frames or an album, then discard the rest.
- Magazines and newspapers: cut out the interesting articles and keep them for reference, then take the rest of them to a recycling center.
- Old videos, records, CDs, and cassette tapes: sell what you can and then discard any old tapes.
- Ornaments: ask yourself why you are keeping gifts or old family items that you don't like. Retain only those that you really love and give away the rest.
- Glasses, bottles of spirits: glasses create positive energy, but not if damaged. Throw out those that are cracked or chipped and discard any bottles that are almost finished.

---

and affection. The danger of hoarding a vast collection of old photographs is that it can link you too strongly to your past. Just keep a few happy pictures of past relationships and dispense with the rest. Make a montage in a glass clipframe of current photos of family and friends. Or display photos of loved ones or happy holidays in metal or wood frames in your relationship or fame areas (see pages 16–17) respectively. Place all other pictures in attractive albums and store neatly in a cabinet.

Magazines and newspapers: These form an ongoing clutter problem that needs constant vigilance. Once you have cut out any articles you want for reference, keep current newspapers and magazines in a magazine rack made from metal, wood, or other combinations. One ingenious cast-iron style has hooped sides to store newspapers flat, allowing string to be put around them for easy removal to a recycling center.

TV, CDs, and DVDs: Easy access is the key for these frequently used items. Feng shui practice dictates that it is preferable to cover a television when it is not in use as it gives off so much yang energy and electromagnetic stress, so

house it in a TV cabinet with doors. DVDs can be stored in a bottom drawer. Slimline CD units are available in various styles; wider units will hold up to 244 CDs. Freestanding metal shelving units are also a good solution for CDs and DVDs.

Ornaments: Place on shelves, or display a favored collection in an illuminated glass cabinet. Clever small cube units (open, with doors, or including shelves) can be mixed and matched to display ornaments, vases, favorite books, and picture frames.

Glasses and bottles: Glasses are very yang and add to the positive energy of the living room. Good-quality glassware looks stunning arranged in a glass cabinet with a wooden frame. Inbuilt downlighters really high-light the sparkle of the glasses.

Soft baskets can hold craft projects (left). Screens can divide multifunctional rooms (above). Candles add yang energy to the living room (right).

Purifying the Soul

Soaking in a hot, relaxing bath or reviving yourself with a quick shower can help you forget all the problems of the day. The bathroom is a place where you can close the door and escape from the outside world—a private retreat for cleansing the body and soul, and somewhere for meditation, contemplation, and inspiration, where ideas are considered and new ones are born. It needs to be a warm and inviting environment where you want to linger—a place that cherishes you.

In a bathroom, water is constantly draining away, making it a very yin environment that

Bathrooms are places where we can escape from the world, so need to be tranquil rooms with clear floors and surfaces.

is prone to stagnation. A surfeit of furniture and messy, overcrowded surfaces will slow down chi energy and stop it circulating properly. The ensuing atmosphere will be stale and the room will make you feel

ENERGY GRIDLOCK

Chi comes into the cluttered bathroom and is blocked by boxes of bathroom products; it then hits the crowded vanity unit and medicine cabinet and is further hindered by clothes on the floor and the mass of beauty items around the bath before it goes out of the window. The flow of chi from the window is interrupted by more products on the bath and towels on the floor before it exits the room.

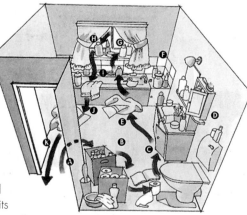

KEY:
A chi enters;
B boxes of bathroom products;
C crowded vanity unit;
D overstocked medicine cabinet;
E clothes on floor;
F overladen bath;
G chi leaves;
H chi comes in window;
I too many bath products;
J wet towels;
K chi leaves

ENERGY FREEWAY

Chi drifts into the well-planned bathroom and around the wicker storage unit and healthy plant, over the bare floor. It goes past the overhauled vanity unit and medicine chest, past an enhancing plant and candles, and out of the window. Chi flowing through the window moves fluently over the smooth bath surfaces, over the mat and towel rail, and exits out of the door.

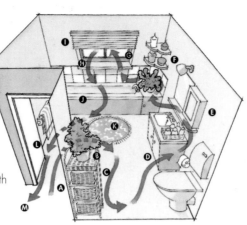

KEY:
A chi enters;
B energizing plant;
C tiered, natural bathroom unit;
D re-worked vanity uni;t
E cleared medicine chest;
F plant and candles for yang energy;
G chi leaves;
H chi comes in window;
I natural blind;
J products moved from bath;
K cotton bath mat;
L heaIed towel rail;
M chi leaves

restless and unsettled. In feng shui terms, bathrooms are not always viewed auspiciously, because water is also linked to money, and this room sees it running away. It is therefore preferable that it is not located in your wealth or career sector. However, they can still be pleasant environments.

THE ENERGY TRAPS

If you find it hard to get in and out of your bathroom because of all the units and baskets, or if you can never find your shampoo, conditioner, or shower gel because they are buried under a mound of other toiletries, you need a thorough cleansing session.

Bathroom cabinets and vanity units: These are good for storage, but if they are packed full of beauty and bathroom items that constantly spill out when you open the doors, making it hard to find what you want to use, you will feel irritated and frustrated.

Beside the sink and bath: A plethora of bottles and tubes, which are guilty of leaving messy deposits in these areas, create a chaotic, disordered feel in a room that should be pleasant and calm. Consider why you feel you need so many.

On the floor: Keeping a stock of toilet paper and cleansers can be a good idea, but if they are stacked on the floor so that you constantly trip over them, they will cause annoyance.

Medicine cabinets: Most creams, tablets, and medicines have a short shelf-life, so check your cabinet to ensure that you don't have expired items. Don't keep unnecessary products that are rarely used—if you do, ask yourself why you are holding onto so many products that only link to ill-health.

A haven of peace

Removing superfluous goods from your bathroom will make you feel better (see checklist), but take a few moments to get a sense of the room that you normally take for granted. It mirrors part of your personality, so do you like what you see? If the paintwork is dirty or peeling, it may indicate a pattern of neglect that you are repeating in your life. Or does its disorder suggest discontentment in your life?

CREATING AN OASIS

Your bathroom should be an oasis where you can refresh body and mind, but if it is a mess, the chi (which is low here anyway) will struggle to work its way through. The stagnancy will drain your energy levels, making you feel constantly tired and listless, and lacking in enthusiasm for life.

COLOR, MOOD, AND LIGHTING

Bathrooms are relaxing rooms, but need to be fed with positive energy to counteract the damp, humid, slightly negative atmosphere that is always present. The color

A bathroom cabinet which is packed full of bathroom products will always irritate you as you won't be able to find anything (left). Regularly remove what you don't need from the cabinet and maybe use baskets inside to maximize the space (below). Painting the bathroom green is very calming and aids digestion.

on the walls also influences your mood. A soft green in a bathroom can aid digestion, while blue, linked to rivers, seas, and lakes, is seen to keep the water in the room flowing swiftly, which is beneficial. Pinks and peaches are calming and soothing.

BATHROOM CLUTTER CHECKLIST

Make your bathroom an enjoyable place to be by first forming your five bags of clutter (see page 33).

- Medicines: check all the use-by dates and throw out accordingly.
- Bathroom cleaners, toilet paper: don't keep enough for an army, just retain a few extra rolls and store your back-up collection elsewhere.

- Bath salts, oils, shower gels, shampoos, and conditioners: are you hoarding a lot of samples? Start working through them, or throw them away. Get rid of any products that are old, dried up, or nearly finished.
- Towels and bath mats: do you have more sets than you need? Are they torn or fraying, or have they seen better days? If so, you know what to do.

Healthy, round-leaved plants will give the room a lift, while using fragrant bath lotions or burning essential oil will clear negativity. Mirrors bring in powerful energy: position one over the sink, keeping it clean and shining. If it becomes tarnished or cracked, replace it immediately as this is bad feng shui and could have adverse effects.

Soft, fluffy towels in pleasing pastel colors will counteract the harder lines of tiled surfaces and the ceramic finishes.

Ceiling downlighters, and task lighting for shaving or applying make-up, will give the right level of brightness. Use scented candles in wall sconces, or safely positioned around the bath to bring in enticing Fire energy.

Leaving wet towels and dirty clothes around the bathroom will further stagnate slow energy (above). This bathroom cabinet (left) can take towels, a small laundry basket, and smaller accessories in the drawers.

Perfect serenity

After you have done a sweep of your bathroom and eliminated everything that's past its best, rethink the way you can best display and store all the essentials in this special room. Bathrooms are often littered with an assortment of bottles of various types of scented gunk, which tend to congregate untidily on window ledges and bath surrounds. The bathroom is often humid and steamy, slowing chi flow, so aim to keep surfaces clear so that the movement of chi is not hindered further.

Towels are better placed in a unit but can sit on shelves when clean and dry.

STORAGE SOLUTIONS

Bath and beauty products:
Generally, these are very attractively packaged, so they look good on open shelving. But do not have too many products on show, just the ones that you regularly use. You can get hanging units to suspend from the shower pipework, which hold shampoo, shower gel, sponges, and soap. Other styles have suction cups that stick to wall tiles. Metal hanging baskets, particularly in a verdigris style, can look stylish. Fit corner shelving into spaces that wouldn't otherwise be used. Glass shelving looks good, and is practical and easy to clean. If you do your make-up in the bathroom, consider buying a unit with drawers that incorporate divided trays with sections for brushes, foundation, lipsticks, and eyeshadows.

Medicines and first-aid kit: These are best hidden away neatly in a wall cabinet. Alternatively, use stacking baskets in a cabinet, or tiered wicker units with pull-out drawers (good for tight spaces).

Bathroom cleaning products: While these are all very necessary, and you may want them on hand rather than in a kitchen cabinet, they clutter and detract from the room if they are left on view. If you lack

space to store them, consider buying a vanity unit to fit around the washbasin. This will utilize the wasted space under the basin and give you at least two extra shelves for storing bulky items such as toilet paper, bleach, disinfectant, and bathroom cleaners. **Towels and bath mats:** Fluffy towels and accessories add a wonderful yin quality to the bathroom. As they are so tactile, extra towels can be put out on display in open

In a large bathroom area, build in as many storage cabinets as you can so that you don't have to leave many goods out. Flowers or plants can raise the chi here.

units—they would look lovely on glass shelves. Alternatively, they can go in glass-fronted units, or in plastic baskets contained in open modern chrome units, mixed in with other baskets of bathroom products (see above).

Creativity and Prosperity

Most of us spend more hours each day in an office environment than we do in our own homes. Even if we work from home, we usually shut the door on our outer family world so that we can get down to work. It is here that we give full rein to our talents for bringing wealth, prosperity, and success into our lives. Clarity and concentration are essential for making the right decisions; we are constantly performing, juggling time and budgets. Here appraisal is constant—all the efforts we make are judged and assessed by bosses, co-workers, and clients.

So, the room you work in should nurture you and your abilities—it should be a pleasant, well-lit, inspiring environment that makes you feel at ease and determined to achieve your best.

The flow of chi in an office must be strong and yang to encourage a positive attitude. If your desk is cluttered and the floor is covered with boxes, reports, and files, chi will get stuck and your creativity and decision-making skills will be blocked, causing you to work in a confused, disorganized way.

THE ENERGY TRAPS

As well as slowing down the chi, an

An ordered office environment will help you think clearly and make decisions more easily.

overcrowded office area restricts the pace of the business, causing misunderstandings and upsets about the current workload.

The desk: Heaps of paperwork awaiting action, files that have not been put away, and unpaid invoices create pools of stagnant energy, making you feel stressed, out of control, and unproductive. If you can never find anything you need in your desk drawers because they are full of irrelevant office equipment, pens that don't work, and old notes, this confusion will make you work sluggishly.

Filing cabinets: When these are overfilled with redundant projects or contain details of bad clients, they make a negative space.

Floor area: If it is an obstacle course of boxes, stacks of files, old reports, and printer paper, these will all restrict energy flow, making the office atmosphere dull.

Cabinets: Bulging office cabinets make people feel oppressed and threatened.

Shelves: Out-of-date catalogs and brochures will just link the business to its past.

Computer: Leaving old material on your machine will hold you back from progressing with new projects.

ENERGY GRIDLOCK

Chi proceeds into the jumbled office and is stopped by an overflowing trash can, files, and a full filing cabinet. It tries to move over a cluttered desk and window ledge before escaping out of the window. Chi streaming in through the window is restricted by too many books on the fax unit and boxes on the floor before leaving the room.

ENERGY FREEWAY

Chi moves into a spring-cleaned office and weaves easily around an emptied filing cabinet and stored files, over the ordered desk space and window ledge and out of the window. The flow of chi back through the window is encouraged by a healthy plant, an uncluttered fax unit, and an empty floor area before leaving the room.

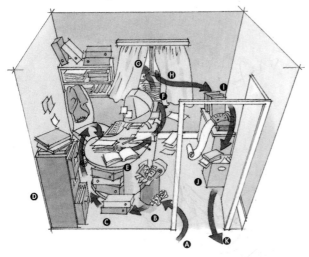

KEY:
A chi enters;
B full trash can;
C box files on floor;
D groaning filing cabinet;
E disorganized desk;
F piles of paperwork;
G chi leaves;
H chi comes in window;
I stacks of books;
J crowded box;
K chi leaves

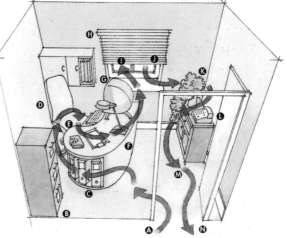

KEY:
A chi enters
B cabinet with current files
C tidy box files
D supportive chair
E efficient desk space
F task light
G clear window ledge
H wooden blind
I chi leaves
J chi enters
K plant to boost atmosphere
L tidy fax unit
M cleared floor
N chi leaves

The work domain

Going through an office and throwing out what's not needed (see checklist) is hard work, so first take a few moments to view your working environment through different eyes. Does it make you feel claustrophobic? Do you feel happy working there, and do its color and lighting work well together, lifting your energy?

WORK ETHICS

To help you work well, the room's atmosphere must encourage productivity. Does the atmosphere feels slow and heavy? If so, it may be a reflection of a business that is run in a rather haphazard way. Consider how your business or company is doing. Has new work decreased or have orders dropped? A disorganized office will dramatically affect the smooth running of a business. Chi will have a problem working its way around the room, and you will feel this hindrance in everything that you attempt—people will always be engaged when you call, important appointments will be canceled, or files will suddenly go missing. If you work at home on your own, and find that you are often restless and unable to sit still or concentrate for long during your working day, it may be because you are surrounded by clutter.

Files, reports, and other papers scattered on the floor will confuse your working practice, so have as many filing cabinets as you can. These Asian wooden ones are also attractive pieces of furniture.

Check to see if cutting chi is coming from sharp corners or shelves and hitting your desk. If so, deflect it with healthy, green, round-leaved plants, or push books to the front of shelves to soften their hard edges. Fresh flowers will lift everyone's mood and raise the energy of the office. Remember to empty all trash cans daily so that you are not surrounded by stagnant energy.

The effects of electromagnetic stress from a computer can be alleviated by taking regular breaks and placing a clear quartz or rose quartz crystal next to it to soak up some of the negative emissions. A cactus called *Cirrus peruvianus* is also good for absorbing the emissions. Peace lilies, peperomias, and dwarf banana plants help cleanse the atmosphere.

In a home office, ideally face south as this is your fame area. Always sit with your back to the wall, for support, and face the door.

COLOR, MOOD, AND LIGHTING

Light cream, white, or pastel colors will increase the space and airiness of an office, or the room can be painted according to the appropriate element (see page 16). Good overhead lighting is important; daylight bulbs, although expensive, help reduce eyestrain as they are the nearest to the ultraviolet light we experience outside. Desk lamps assist close reading and computer work.

Sunlight introduces warmth and yang energy, but can be blinding and create irritating glare on computers, even in winter, so venetian blinds at the windows are essential. To reduce glare, position your desk so that windows are at the side of it. If you cannot avoid glare, hang a faceted spherical crystal (see page 92) in the window to dispel the negative chi from the glare.

Successful placement

The position of your desk can affect your work efficiency and achievements. The best position, in feng shui terms, is in the corner that is diagonally opposite the main door of your office. You need to be able to see the door and who is coming into the room. If you sit with your back to the door, you will always feel threatened, or that other colleagues are betraying you. However, if sitting like this is unavoidable, hang a small mirror over your desk so that you see the door behind youreflected in it.

Your chair should always have a solid wall, rather than a window, behind it, because this gives you symbolic support. If you have no choice but to sit with a window behind you, then keep the blind down—doing this symbolizes a measure of support. Also, avoid sitting too close to the office door, because it will make you feel that you are unprotected and that you are losing control.

Tall, slim filing cabinets can be slotted into narrow spaces in the office.

SITING A HOME OFFICE

An ideal position for your home office (if you are running a business) is facing south, because this governs your fame area. Situate a home study to face the northeast, which relates to your education and knowledge area. If these positions are not possible, use your compass (see page 17) and place your desk in a south or northeast corner.

AN OPEN-PLAN OFFICE

When several members of staff share an open-plan office, it is better to get a feng shui consultant in to map it out and ascertain the best positions for people to sit. Alternatively, use the compass and Pa Kua and from your readings work out the most auspicious areas for computers, fax machines, and filing cabinets. You can also follow some general guidelines. The most favorable position for the manager's office is farthest from the office door, so that he or she is apart from the bustle of the office, and is able to make decisions without distractions, promoting good control over the business. You should not

If your desk is constantly in a mess, you will work in a distracted, unstructured way and will be forever losing files, invoices, and vital reports and notes. Try to address correspondence as soon as it comes in or make your comments and pass it on. The aim at the end of the day is to leave an empty, tidy desk—this is not always easy to achieve, but it is something to aim for.

place desks facing each other because this can sometimes cause confrontation between colleagues.

Computer disks and small stationery items such as staples, paperclips, erasers, and pens and pencils can be put in this small unit (below).

OFFICE CLUTTER CHECKLIST

Although clearing out office clutter is slightly different from sorting out the home, you can still work through the five-bag system (see page 33).

- Files: sort through your filing cabinets and throw out redundant files, keeping only the current ones.

- Catalogs, reference magazines, and brochures: send old ones for recycling.

- Reference books: keep up-to-date books with the latest information, and give the rest away.

- Reports: retain reference copies of old reports and shred the rest.

- Desk: transfer messages or Post-it notes to your diary, and junk any irrelevant pieces of paper crowding the desk.

- Computer: go through the hard disk and put disused programs, completed or abandoned projects, and emails on a back-up disk or archiving system, or throw them away.

Inspired filing

Now that you have started taking action in your home office or your place of work, by removing waste and clutter, you need to evaluate how to make better use of your space so that it doesn't become a mess again. See if there is room for more filing cabinets to consume paperwork or files stacked on the floor. Is it necessary to buy another cabinet for stationery? Perhaps an alcove can be utilized by building in more shelves for reference books.

Stationery trays need not be only metal or plastic but can also be made from natural fibers, which are especially good for chi movement (left).

If you do not have too many files, these storage boxes will be perfectly adequate (above).

STORAGE SOLUTIONS

Files: If your company has numerous projects running at one time, with related files, it is worth installing tall, metal file cabinets that feature several shelves of hanging files. Box files can be stored in smaller versions with deeper shelves.

Alternatively, incorporate conventional metal file cabinets with two, three, or four pull-out drawers. To boost the Metal element, place these in the west of the office. In a home office, there is usually a less pressing demand for filing space, and attractive wooden or melamine units with one filing drawer and two storage drawers will suffice. Buy one that is on rollers, so it will slide under a desk. Some computer desk units have a pull-out keyboard shelf and extra shelves for computer accessories and manuals.

Stationery: This can easily get out of control, so if your present cabinet is inadequate, invest in furniture to contain it, such as a tall metal unit with three shelves and lockable doors. Smaller cabinets with one shelf are also available. A slimline multi-drawer cabinet can adequately hold business stationery. Compartmentalized insert trays can be added for loose items such as paperclips, pens, and markers. For home use, stylish plastic pull-out drawer units on rollers will absorb various pieces of stationery. Stacking boxes in transparent plastic look good sitting on shelves, and will hold disks, CDs, and index cards.

If you are on a tight budget, these inexpensive cardboard boxes will hold different items.

Printer paper: Rather than leaving packs of paper lying on the floor, improve matters with a cabinet where the printer sits on top and paper is stored on shelves in the cabinet below.

Catalogs, brochures, and reports: Use box files for these and label clearly. Store them on open metal or wooden shelving units, bringing the files to the edge to stop the sharp edges creating cutting chi. Or they can be secreted in stackable modular units with pulldown doors. In the home office, transparent plastic lidded stacking boxes or plastic magazine holders will keep brochures or catalogs stored neatly.

Reference books: Stand in rows on open metal or wood shelving units as above, but never position a unit behind a desk because it can send out cutting chi. Ideally, look for a unit with deep shelves fitted with doors to counteract this problem, or use freestanding cabinets with several shelves and glass or wooden doors.

Where Memories Live On

All too often, the attic becomes a memorial junkyard to our past. We seem to feel that this space above us can symbolically oppress us with our past emotions—our elation at success in school or sport, our sadness at the loss of relatives or failure in various projects. It encompasses the pain and passion of love affairs, the pride and unconditional love of parenthood. The past spirit of the home seems to rest here, lingering over the family like a murky cloud. The loft can also be a repository for feelings of disapproval and dislike, as we secrete more and more unwanted gifts in this deep, dark space.

The flow of energy through this higher storage area is naturally sluggish as there tends to be little ventilation. However, it is important that chi is able to move—if the attic is full with junk, it will struggle to move at all, and become an inhibiting heaviness that looms over the house.

If your room is like this, consider why you feel you need to hold on to so many reminders of your past—are you worried or frightened about what the future might hold?

THE ENERGY TRAPS

Inevitably, the attic is the area that holds many different possessions, but it is what is placed here and how it is stored that really matters. Overloading your attic with too much junk can symbolically restrict your higher achievements and aims, and it

ENERGY GRIDLOCK

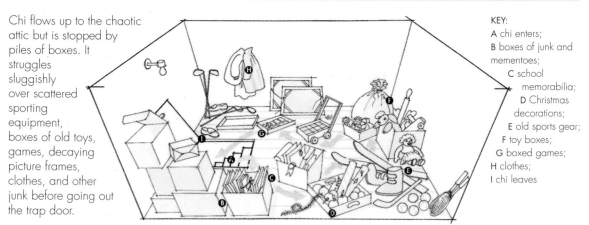

Chi flows up to the chaotic attic but is stopped by piles of boxes. It struggles sluggishly over scattered sporting equipment, boxes of old toys, games, decaying picture frames, clothes, and other junk before going out the trap door.

KEY:
A chi enters;
B boxes of junk and mementoes;
C school memorabilia;
D Christmas decorations;
E old sports gear;
F toy boxes;
G boxed games;
H clothes;
I chi leaves

ENERGY FREEWAY

Chi travels into the overhauled attic, moving freely around storage boxes, a shoe rack, other boxed items, sporting equipment, rarely used jackets, home repair tools, stored games and sports gear to leave by the trap door.

KEY:
A chi enters;
B mementoes box;
C ordered shoe rack;
D labeled storage boxes;
E ski bag;
F rack with outdoor jackets;
G home repair unit;
H storage rack for games and sports items;
I chi leaves

can create a subconscious fear of what the future may bring.

Empty boxes: It always seems a good idea to keep these in case they come in useful for something. However, they waste space and give out stagnant energy. Select several sturdy boxes for emergencies, remove any staples carefully, and fold them flat.

School memorabilia: Boxes of old school books, lesson notes, certificates, and awards drag you down. Even if you are proud of your achievements, they are still linking you inexorably with your past.

Boxes of romantic mementoes: Aging, dusty love letters tied in ribbon, along with other special mementoes that remind you of past relationships, cannot help but give off a musty, sad energy that can be difficult to shift.

Board games and cards: Stacks of old games and cards, once played every Christmas and holiday, but now hardly used, create dull, stuck energy.

Old appliances, sports and fitness equipment: Cumbersome, rusting equipment takes up space in the attic and will probably never be used again. Its bulky presence only causes you irritation and annoyance.

Family memorabilia: Boxes containing reminders of everything that your children ever achieved at school or university again pull you back to the past, restricting new, exciting growth ahead.

Boxes of miscellaneous items: A dumping ground for unwanted or discarded items that you never got around to sorting out, this cache of unresolved mess can make you feel stuck and may cause depression.

A refuge for the past

Clearing out this room is an arduous task, so before you start, assess the extent of the problem (see checklist). If it is dull and musty and so crowded with articles associated with your past life that you cannot move around easily, you must loosen your grip on the past.

PRESSURE FROM ABOVE

New experiences won't be able to come into your life until you let go of the old ones symbolized by all the outgrown possessions and mementoes stored here. By tying

yourself to the unwanted and unused, you have allowed sentiment to restrict you like a ball and chain. Sloping ceilings will add to the feeling of pressure and being compressed that the attic creates for members of the household.

COLOR, MOOD, AND LIGHTING

The energy in an attic is very yin and passive and will have a natural tendency to stagnate because normally there are no windows—no outlets—for it to escape through. Light cream, yellow, or pastel shades of paint will help to make the room brighter and more appealing. Although it is not worth spending a lot on lighting, putting in some spotlights or bulkhead lighting will help to lift the dull energy.

All too often, our past life seems to be stored in the attic (far left) and we hang on to too many sentimental papers (left). Be ruthless and keep only what you really want on efficient shelving units such as these (above).

Re-designed space

You may feel exhausted after clearing out the attic, because it contained so many extraneous items from the past, but you now need storage systems for everything that qualifies living there. Plan carefully, as this area can easily become cluttered again, slowing down energy that already struggles to flow freely. Put the items you need to access most frequently near the attic hatch. Create organized space with planned shelving units and durable storage boxes, and you will allow calming energy to float down into the rest of the house.

Basic shelving units are easy to buy and can take care of bulky ski boots or walking shoes. Skis can be stored next to them or in protective ski bags.

ATTIC CLUTTER CHECKLIST

Search through all the junk from your past, sorting it into different piles for the five-bag system (see page 33).

- Boxes: these seem so useful but just sit there collecting dust, so throw them out. Keep appliance boxes for the guarantee period and then get rid of them.

- Schoolbooks, clothes, diplomas, medals, and sashes: you know your achievements, so dump these links to your youth.

- Games and cards: keep the ones that are still used, and give the rest to a hospital or a children's home.

- Love letters, dried flowers, old cards: if you can't bear to part with all of them, keep a few really special items and throw away the rest.

- Old equipment such as exercise bikes, baseball bats, and footballs: admit to yourself that these will never be used again, and throw out or donate to sports clubs.

- Christmas and other holiday decorations: discard damaged items and wrinkled pieces of tinsel.

STORAGE SOLUTIONS

Games and card sets: Stack favorites neatly on shelving units, putting card packs in small cardboard boxes. If there is enough height for freestanding wooden or metal units with wide shelves, these will accommodate a lot of items, otherwise single melamine or wooden shelves on metal struts are a good budget solution.

Love memorabilia: Choose a special wicker, rattan, natural fiber, or leather box for these precious mementoes, so that it emphasizes the love that you still feel for them. Put it somewhere that is easy to reach, so if you are in a sentimental mood you can get it down to have another look at your treasures.

Ski clothes, sports clothes, and hiking or walking jackets: Put in plastic garment bags to protect them from dirt and dust and hang on clothing rails, or store tidily in large, labeled plastic boxes.

Walking or hiking boots: Clean well and store on sturdy shoe

Hardwearing boxes on wheels are ideal for the attic as they can be easily moved around.

racks or in large hanging units suspended from a hook in the wall.

Decorations, gardening, and home repair equipment, and miscellaneous items: Place these in solid plastic or substantial cardboard stacking boxes with lids and label the contents clearly. Store them in relevant groups, stacked one on top of each other, taking care to make them accessible. Tiny accessories, screws, nails, or other small home repair items can be put into different-sized chest units, with small, labeled pull-out drawers, made from plywood or a similar inexpensive wood.

Place your love letters in an appealing box that you will cherish.

Clutter on the Move

A car can be very much an extension of our personalities—a mobile possession that projects another part of us. So much time is spent in our cars traveling to and from destinations that we form a strong, almost emotional, attachment to it. We choose it partly because of the appeal of its color, style, design, and look. It is our own private little world, where we want to feel safe and secure.

While driving, it is obviously important to stay bright and alert, so the chi in the car needs to be positive and very yang. If your car is a trash can on wheels, the chi will find it difficult to flow around strongly. This can have a profound effect, slowing your reactions and decision-making skills and causing you to drive in a less assured way.

THE ENERGY TRAPS

Hoarding things in your car will affect you as much as amassing junk in your home, because you are recreating this disturbed energy on the move. A good clear-out will bring about a major energy shift.

In the trunk: This area can become a black hole where piles of articles such as shoes, jackets, or sports items are all dumped. This will only become a mass of heavy energy, which may tend to disturb

ENERGY GRIDLOCK

Chi flows into the junk-filled car and is obstructed by parking tickets, receipts, and discarded CDs. It tries to move over thrown food packaging, toys, and atlases before exiting. In the trunk, chi then has problems working around a scrunched up rug, jackets, sports shoes, and car accessories before leaving.

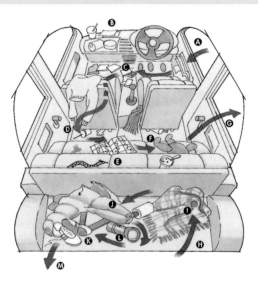

KEY:
A chi enters;
B parking tickets, receipts, and other paper;
C piles of CDs;
D food and drink cartons;
E dumped atlases;
F abandoned toys;
G chi leaves;
H chi enters trunk;
I messy rug;
J piles of jackets;
K training shoes;
L car accessories;
M chi leaves

your concentration while you are driving around.

Door pockets and compartments: Can you never find the map you want because there is so much crammed in these storage sections? This sort of clutter can cloud your thinking, making you feel confused.

Seats: Are you embarrassed to offer a friend a lift because there is hardly any space to sit down? Are CDs, empty bottles, and parking tickets scattered over seats and floor? Can you never get the seats forward to let people in because of junk stuffed behind them? This type of disorder may well reflect how you organize your life.

A car is an important possession for most of us, and, like our homes, needs to be regularly assessed for clutter, because this slows the chi movement inside it, which can adversely affect our driving skills.

ENERGY FREEWAY

Chi moves into the spruced up car, proceeds evenly around the CD box and cleared floor into the back over cleaned seats, stored road books, and trash can and out of the window. Chi comes into the trunk and circulates well around the storage box and car rug before leaving.

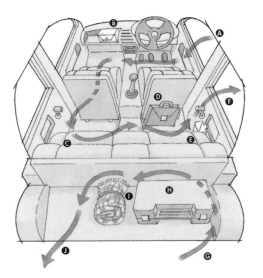

KEY:
A chi enters;
B CD storage box;
C cleaned seats;
D atlas storage case;
E hanging trash can;
F chi leaves;
G chi enters trunk;
H car accessory box;
I neatly rolled rug;
J chi leaves

A world on the move

Sorting out your car's junk will be a huge relief, but before you get started (see checklist), stand back and look at your car. Do you feel pride when you look at it? Or do you feel ashamed because it is so dirty and shabby? Remember that in feng shui, it is believed that what is going on in our outer life is reflected inside us.

COLOR AND ATMOSPHERE

Color has a strong influence on us, so the color of your car will affect how you behave when you're on the road. In feng shui terms, red is yang and therefore very stimulating, sometimes causing anger and irritability, so this may well make you drive faster or rather aggressively. Yellow is uplifting and encourages an optimistic attitude while driving. Blue and green are calming, as they are more yin (passive) colors, and will create a relaxed atmosphere for driving. Black or gray are very yin; black will give comfort and protection in a car, while gray encourages self-reliance. White and silver are very yang colors—white gives protection, while silver promotes harmony and balance when traveling.

Dust and dirt will taint the atmosphere inside a car, so clean it out regularly. Interior surfaces are often plastic and therefore yang. If they are gray, they will shield you from outside influences. Fabric and leather seats are yin, and their softness

Tidy away regularly used items in the door pockets of your car, rather than leaving them on the seats.

counteracts the hard yang lines of the plastic. As always, good feng shui requires a balance of yin and yang energies, so there needs to be an equal presence of these two in your car.

Keep all your favorite music for the car in a handy CD box.

STORAGE SOLUTIONS

Road maps and atlases: Keep these in the door pockets rather than on or under the seat, or if you have a lot of them, store them together in a clean plastic briefcase, and place this tidily behind a seat.

CDs and books: Place these in plastic storage boxes or padded zipped cases which can be stored in the glove compartment or on the back seat.

Trash: If you really can't keep this under control, place a small plastic trash can in the car and empty it regularly. Some styles hook on to the car doors.

Miscellaneous car items: Put car oil, jumper cables, the tire pump, and other useful car accessories into a sturdy plastic storage box. Make sure it is an adequate size for your needs and comes with a lid so that items don't rattle around loose in the trunk.

CAR CLUTTER CHECKLIST

If your car is a mess, get some garbage bags to remove the junk.

- Road maps, atlases: search through these carefully, discard out-of-date versions, and give away maps that are no longer needed.
- Food wrappers, cartons, empty bottles, parking tickets: search out and destroy all this stagnant energy.
- CDs and story tapes: keep a select few of your favorites, change these regularly to create new energy, and take the rest back into the house.
- Shoes, coats, sports gear, miscellaneous car items: these are generating stale energy, so remove them and store indoors.

The Walking Clutter Mountain

I f clutter has invaded your home and car, it is likely this chaos has spread to the possessions that you carry around with you.

PURSES (HANDBAGS)

These are very personal items, chosen with care. They show part of our personalities, and are linked to the overall style that we like to present to other people. So why do so many of us fill them up with useless articles?

If you are trying to portray a positive, confident, organized attitude, owning a bulging, overloaded purse reveals that there are areas of disorder in your life.

Contents overload: Scribbled notes and phone numbers, receipts, old shopping lists, vouchers, bills, numerous pens that don't work, several hairbrushes, and old make-up—all these slow you down by creating pools of dull energy.

Rather than keeping new phone numbers on scraps of paper, transfer them to your Filofax or personal organizer.

Solutions: Sort through your bag, throwing away useless papers and pens, and transfer phone numbers to your address book, Filofax, or personal organizer. Dispense with old make-up, keep current items in a neat make-up bag, and retain one hairbrush. Remove receipts and vouchers and file in a plastic folder with sections—review regularly and discard them when no longer needed.

COINPURSES AND WALLETS

Overcrowding these with extraneous matter can have a negative effect on your finances.

Contents overload: Old business cards, out-of-date credit cards, membership cards, appointment cards, and credit card vouchers can all drain your finances.

Solutions: Take out the business cards and record useful contact details in your address book, write appointments in your diary, and cut up expired credit and membership cards. File credit card vouchers in a folder and review monthly to keep in order.

BRIEFCASES

Like purses, briefcases reflect your character, and contribute to your outward impression.

Even if you are dressed smartly, a crammed, shabby briefcase will indicate disorder and lack of control.

Contents overload: Old files, memos, unread reports, unanswered correspondence, broken pens and pencils, reference books—these slow you down and bring in chaos.

An ordered briefcase will help you stay in control of your working life (above). Keep paper to the minimum by transferring addresses to your address book and appointments to your diary (left).

Solutions: Note the contents of memos then throw them away. Remove files that you don't need and put them back in the office. Create an office action folder for letters. Read reports then return them to the office. Throw out old stationery and keep a couple of working pens in a pocket in your briefcase. Return reference books to their sources. Resolve from now on to carry only the paperwork that you need for meetings or working at home.

Energize with Feng Shui Cures

It's taken time, but you've finally got to grips with your clutter and worked through the emotional loss of throwing away belongings that you have become attached to over the years. You've also done a space-clearing ceremony to release any trapped negative energies that may still be clinging to your home, but what next? Perhaps the atmosphere around you still feels a bit dull and in need of a lift. For a thorough feng shui analysis, you need the services of a consultant, who can harmonize the home's energies and the surrounding environment. But there are also some simple feng

shui enhancements and cures, detailed here, that you can apply yourself in order to raise your home's energy vibrations and make it a brighter, more appealing place to live.

HOW DO THEY WORK?

Enhancements boost the energy around the eight life aspiration areas of the Pa Kua (see pages 16–17), such as your relationship or wealth corner. Cures can be carefully positioned to offset any problems or correct negative energy affecting the room's atmosphere. For example, healthy plants are positive

Candlelight is always inspiring and brings in positive yang energy to a room.

and yang, and they can be used to shield people against harmful cutting chi emanating from a corner or pillar. Plants can also lessen the effects of electromagnetic stress that come from a television or other electrical equipment in the home.

By harmonizing the energies in each room, you will feel your home start to come alive again and work positively for you.

WHAT CAN YOU USE?

There are several different types of feng shui cure and enhancement that can be placed around your home:

- Mirrors lift energy and expand spaces, but must be used with caution in the bedroom.
- The soft, tinkly sound of wind chimes is either used to slow down the flow of chi or encourage its circulation in the home.
- Crystals have a strong vibrational energy and their uses include activating the career area, healing, and attracting more energy into a room.
- Water features or aquariums encourage money to flow into your life when placed in your wealth area.
- Lights or candles bring strong yang energy to stagnant areas, or can raise the energy in your fame section.
- Plants are versatile feng shui cures. Their healthy, positive energy can help alleviate problem areas.
- Attaching bamboo flutes to overhead beams reduces their negative impact.
- Metal and electrical items enhance the energy of the west.
- Paired items represent togetherness and romance and can strengthen an existing relationship or entice new partners.
- Mirrors shaped like the Pa Kua, situated outside the home by the front door, help to deflect bad energy attacking the home.

MIRRORS

In the past, mirrors were considered so special that only people such as pharaohs, kings, and shamans were allowed to use them. In feng shui, mirrors are powerful tools. A flat mirror expands energy, and will open up a narrow space such as a hall, lightening the area and creating the illusion of more space.

Symbolically, a mirror can also "double" energy. So if it is placed opposite a dining table, for example, it "doubles" the value of the food on the table, and is believed to increase the family's wealth. However, don't put a mirror opposite your cluttered desk, because it will double your workload.

Mirrors also serve the symbolic purpose of making things "disappear." So if your toilet faces the front door, which according to feng shui is a very bad position, putting a mirror on the toilet door will in effect make it "disappear." Another function of mirrors is to deal with irregularly shaped rooms, which are believed to be inauspicious as they have a section of the Pa Kua missing. A "missing corner" can be reinstated by using a mirror.

A mirror is very yang, so in a bathroom can help to lift the slow energy that exists there.

For example, if there is a missing corner in the career area, place a mirror facing inward on one wall of the L-shape to symbolically restore it.

It is possible to buy eight-sided mirrors shaped like the Pa Kua. These are very powerful, so use them carefully. Never place a Pa Kua mirror inside the home; instead, hang it outside your front door to fend off bad energies, such as cutting chi coming from a road directly opposite. But position it with care, making sure that it does not reflect neighboring homes and send bad energy to them.

Mirror lore

- Never position mirrors facing each other, because they will bounce chi back and forth.
- Don't use a cracked or tarnished mirror as it literally and symbolically will distort your image.
- Keep mirrors sparkling clean. When not in use, store face down, otherwise they can bring confusion into your life.
- Do not hang a mirror to reflect your bed, because its energy can cause restlessness and insomnia.
- Never place a mirror opposite your front door, because it will send the good energy that enters out again.

A metal wind chime can lift the chi in the west of a room.

WIND CHIMES

In ancient China, wind chimes were traditionally hung to frighten away unsettled spirits. But nowadays in modern feng shui they have a more positive influence in the home. When a wind chime is positioned inside a front door that opens opposite a staircase, for example, incoming chi that would otherwise rush straight up the stairs is filtered and slowed down by the beautiful tinkling chimes. Hung inside or outside, wind chimes ward off negative forces, activate chi, and raise chi in a dull area.

Suspended outside the front door, a melodious five-rod metal windchime can deflect cutting chi coming off the corners of other buildings.

When trying to choose a wind chime to lift energy in a room, first of all, find out the room's direction and element so that you know whether you need to hang metal, ceramic, or wooden wind chimes. In the west (Metal), northwest (Metal), and north (Water is produced by Metal), metal wind chimes are best. Ceramic chimes will suit the southwest (Earth) and northeast (Earth). Wooden chimes work particularly well in the east (Wood), southeast (Wood), and south (the Fire element is produced by Wood).

CRYSTALS

A small, sparkling, lead-faceted crystal sphere dangling in a sunny window spreads an inspiring rainbow of beautiful colors across the walls. Everyone will notice its uplifting effect as it raises the energy vibrations of the room. If you position it in a specific area of the Pa Kua, it will bring extra energy to that sector. In your wealth area, for example, you will notice that your bank balance stays healthy and that money seems to come your way more easily.

Crystals are good for energizing areas of your home. Natural quartz (see opposite) can boost your relationship corner in the southwest of your living room.

Hang or place a crystal in a room, after clutter has been cleared out, to create a significant shift in energy flow. Crystals also reduce negativity, deflecting cutting chi aimed at the house by telegraph poles or bus stops. A 1in (20mm) sphere is the right size for activating a small room, while a 1½in (30mm) crystal is better for an average room. Hang the crystal near the top of the window in the center of a pane.

If you are seeking a new relationship, or if an existing one needs some help, a powerful natural quartz cluster can energize the southwest (relationship) corner of your lounge, while an amethyst crystal will stimulate the northeast (education and knowledge) sector.

Rose quartz is associated with romance, so again place in the southwest. Its soothing qualities will also calm disruptive children, if it is placed in their bedroom.

Crystal tips

- Cleanse new crystals briefly under cold water. If they were bought in a big crystal shop, soak for 24 hours to remove other energies.
- Clean hanging crystals weekly by dipping in still spring mineral water and leaving to dry.
- To activate the powers of a crystal, mentally state your intention for it when you hang it up.
- Amethyst is a wonderful healing stone. Use it to aid recovery from illness.

WATER FEATURES

The trickling sound of flowing water is soothing. Water is a wonderful carrier of chi, and it can entice positive energy into your home. Water is also traditionally associated with wealth by the Chinese.

The best place for an indoor water feature is the southeast (Wood and wealth) corner of your home or lounge. This is because in the cycle of the five elements, Water

produces Wood. Choose a small indoor fountain, a trickling water feature, or an aquarium. It is preferable to have an odd number of fish in an aquarium, with nine considered to be very lucky. Ideally, one should be a different color to absorb negative energy, so eight orange goldfish and one black one would be a good combination. The constant motion of the oxygenated water and the fish stimulate the chi in the water. A pond or a small fountain on the left-hand side of your front garden encourages the flow of good energy to your home. Fountains also deflect any cutting chi that is adversely affecting your home. Keep water clean and fresh to avoid the pitfalls of stagnancy.

Do not put a water feature or image of water in your bedroom, because Water overwhelms Earth in the element cycle (and the bedroom is considered to be Earth). A surfeit of Water is thought to cause relationship problems.

LIGHTING

Lights can bathe a room in soft, warm light, provide localized light for reading, or dramatically light a dinner table. They affect our moods, stimulating or relaxing us.

Contemporary lighting is an integral part of interior design and also plays an important part in feng shui. Lights link to the Fire element, bringing positive yang energy to every room. They encourage the flow of chi, particularly in the south. Carefully planned lighting creates balance and harmony.

Where possible, choose table and floor lamps that relate to the element of the areas where they are being placed. For example, rounded, oval, or dome shapes work best in the west and northwest, which link to Metal. Tall, straight lights are appropriate for the east and southeast sections that relate to Wood. Flowing, wavy, or irregular shapes are associated with Water and will enhance areas in the north.

Soft candlelight can promote a relaxing ambience in a room.

CANDLES

Soft, flickering candles bring a natural light and yang energy, and add a special atmosphere to a living or dining room. In the bedroom, candles give off a soft light, creating a gentle aura of romance.

Bathrooms are usually steamy and humid, therefore the energy here will be very slow-moving. Plain or scented candles situated by the bathtub or in wall sconces lift this energy while imbuing the area with a warm, ambient glow—ideal for a room where we need to feel completely relaxed.

PLANTS

Healthy green plants are living feng shui enhancements that give out oxygen, generating a special chi that engenders a fresher, lively atmosphere. As energizers, they lift stagnant energy in dark corners, and when sited near electrical equipment they counterbalance negative electromagnetic fields. They have the ability to remove toxins from the air, can obscure cutting chi from sharp-angled furniture or columns, and can slow down chi that moves too fast down a long corridor.

However, the shape of a plant's leaves is important. Spiky-leaved plants are believed to send out bad chi from their sharp leaves, so choose varieties with rounded, succulent leaves to attract auspicious chi.

Burning candles in the bedroom brings a romantic feel to this tranquil room.

In the bathroom, plants will absorb humidity and raise chi levels, while in a kitchen they are able to increase the existing yang energy. However, do not place them near the stove, because their Wood element will fuel the Fire energy of the stove too much.

In order to enhance and strengthen the Wood element in your home, you can site plants in the east (associated with family and health) and the southeast (linked with wealth and prosperity). A money plant in your wealth area is believed to mirror your fortunes according to how well it grows. Plants can also boost corners in the south of your home (representing Fire, fame, and recognition), because Wood feeds Fire in the cycle of elements.

part two

the declutter projects

The Hall Challenge

TO MAKE AN ENTRANCE: 5 HOURS

Step 1—Complete the questionnaire (see pages 150–151) and prepare yourself

Step 2—Look at your entrance/hall

Step 3—Clear the doorway

Step 4—Sort your pictures

Step 5—Review your mirrors

Step 6—Search through junk mail and keys

Steps 7 & 8—Your affirmation for success

STEP 1 GETTING STARTED

Fill in the questionnaire on pages 150–151 to assess your clutter problem. Do as much as you can cope with, but don't ever feel you haven't achieved enough. Locate your worst junk heaps, asking yourself questions such as:

● Can I easily open my front door?

● Do I have hoards of shoes and outdoor clothes lying in a heap?

● Are there always piles of old magazines and newspapers waiting to be removed?

Tackle the worst pile in each area first.

STEP 2 FOR AN INVITING ATMOSPHERE

Think about how it feels when you enter your home. Do you often feel irritated when you first come in? Are mountains of junk obstructing the entrance, so that it's always untidy and

disordered? (Check your questionnaire answers.) Your entrance and hall welcomes people into your home, so these areas need to be vibrant and appealing. If chi (energy) can't enter easily, it slows down, creating a stifling atmosphere. Ask yourself if you are subliminally stopping people from visiting you. Write down how you want your hall to look.

STEP 3 THE DOORWAY

Check for:

✓ Shoes, boots

✓ Snow boots

✓ Jackets/coats, scarves, hats

✓ Strollers (pushchairs)

✓ Umbrellas (working and broken)

✓ Boxes of junk

✓ Bicycles, golf clubs

✓ Work bags/briefcases

This area can be a virtual dumping ground as the family come home and discards their items of the day. If it is not tackled straight away, people will feel pushed out by the disorder.

Get organized: Throw out obvious junk and broken objects; add more coatstands or closets for outdoor clothes; get a shoe tree/rack; ask for sports gear to be put away in relevant closets or the shed; store bikes in garage or shed; put work items neatly at side or in home office.

Maintenance: Spend ten minutes daily sorting out clutter that has crept back. Consider fining every household member a small amount for charity if they lapse into untidy habits.

Obvious benefits of clear-out
You can easily open the door into a bright, clean hall.

Emotional benefits of clear-out
A black cloud lifts from you mentally, you feel happier entering your home.

STEP 4 PICTURES

Check for:

✓ Vacation posters or enlarged photographs

✓ Female/male pictures

   ✓ Frightening abstracts or masks

   ✓ Sad, gloomy art

Study your hall pictures. Do you still like them? Our energy changes as we get older and so do our preferences—we all need new stimuli to represent the person we are becoming.

If you're a single woman and have pictures everywhere of single women, you are saying that's the way you want to stay. If your pictures or masks are sad or frightening, what is that saying about your enjoyment of life? Posters or photos of a brilliant vacation have a short lifespan, so enjoy them for a while and then make a change.

Your hall should be an inviting place, free of clutter, that welcomes people in.

Obvious benefits of clear-out
Your pictures get dusted and your walls cleaned as you move everything around.

Emotional benefits of clear-out
You will feel much happier with inspiring pictures that depict what you like and want now.

Get organized: Discard old posters and photos, and offputting art; balance male/female art. Show pictures of happy couples to boost relationships or encourage them. Display recent photos.

Maintenance: Make minor changes every six months; bring in new art yearly.

STEP 5 MIRRORS

Check for:

✔ Cracked, discolored mirrors

✔ Mirrors that distort

✔ Mirrors propped up in the hall

✔ Mirrors facing the door

In feng shui, mirrors are very yang, or powerful, so use them sparingly. They can light up or expand halls, but if you display damaged mirrors, think about why you are trying to distort your vision of life.

Get organized: Discard damaged mirrors now; cover and store unused ones to prevent energy bouncing around. Clean a new mirror regularly so it reflects well. Never place a mirror opposite the front door (energy goes out again) or have two mirrors opposite each other—it creates energetic confusion.

Obvious benefits of clear-out
A brighter, sparkling hall.

Emotional benefits of clear-out
A positive energy-blast when you enter your home.

Maintenance: Check every six months for any cracks or signs of wear.

STEP 6 JUNK MAIL AND KEYS

Check for:

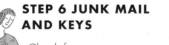

✔ Advertising leaflets, unopened credit card or charity envelopes, take-out menus, taxicab cards

✔ Odd keys

The amount of mail that comes into our homes daily is phenomenal. Sticking it in a drawer or letting it pile up behind the door makes hidden piles of stale energy that will start to irritate you. And what about discarded keys from old locks, homes, or cars? Why do you hold on to items or places that are no longer a part of your life?

Get organized: Keep useful advertising, take-out leaflets, and taxi cards on a pinboard or in a folder. Discard the rest with unwanted charity or credit card information. Keep current keys and hang on hooks.

Obvious benefits of clear-out
You can enter your home without tripping over a paper mound.

Emotional benefits of clear-out
An ordered hall means an ordered mind.

Maintenance: Check leaflets weekly to stop the pile building again. When you have a new lock, car, home, or lockable item, dispense with old keys.

SUMMARY

Well done. Praise yourself for what you've achieved and see how good you feel. If you didn't manage to do all the tasks you wanted, just allocate some extra time to finish them.

Welcoming entrance

STEP 7 HALL REWARDS

Check for:

✓ Removing junk from the doorway

✓ Rationalizing your art

✓ Replacing broken mirrors

✓ Removing old junk mail and keys

This is an important area to keep clear, as this is where people get a first impression of your home. If you have managed at least two of the above goals, you are succeeding in de-junking this space. Allow yourself a couple of the treats below, or make your own choice.

Clear-out treats

● A bunch of scented seasonal flowers for the hall table

● An attractive pinboard

● A bright rug that welcomes people in

● A new piece of art

● A new umbrella stand

● A mirror or a new picture light

STEP 8 YOUR WISH CARD

Before you finish your clear-out, choose a photocopy of the card on page 176. Write down your wish for your ultimate hall, or choose one of the following.

"I choose a light and airy hall."

"I want a hall with pictures that lift my soul."

"I desire a hall that visitors love to enter."

"I would like a hall that is the delightful entrance to my sanctuary."

"I crave a hall with neat, ordered storage."

REAL-LIFE LETTING GO

I was working on the hall during a decluttering consultation in Patricia's apartment when I came across the junk drawer in her table there. As I rummaged through it, discarding notes and unused leaflets, I found a set of keys hidden at the back. When I showed them to Patricia, she looked a bit embarrassed as she admitted they were from a home that she had owned five years ago. She told me how she had found it hard to settle in her current home, and her keys were her way of hanging onto a loved property. I got her to throw out her old apartment keys, and a few weeks later she rang to say that she felt much more secure.

The Kitchen Challenge

FOR A ROOM OF NOURISHMENT: 5½ HOURS

Step 9—Complete the questionnaire (see pages 150–151) and look at the kitchen

Step 10—Cut back on seasonings, sauces, and spices

Step 11—Hunt for unused appliances

Step 12—Examine the contents of your refrigerator/freezer

Step 13—Search through cabinets for any damaged china

Step 14—Sort out the trash and unused plastic bags

Steps 15 & 16—Your affirmation for success

STEP 9 MAKING A ROOM FOR HEALTHY EATING

Look around your kitchen.
What are your feelings and first impressions about this room—is it the healthy, cozy haven it should be? (Check back on your answers to the questionnaire.) Or does it present a clutter disaster zone? Now ask yourself the following questions:

● Are your cabinets packed full of food or seasonings that are never used?

● Is there unknown food lurking in your refrigerator/freezer?

● Have you found unused appliances hidden away in corners?

● Are corners of your kitchen stuffed with old plastic bags or paper bags?

This is a room where food is prepared and eaten. It is the "heart" of the home, needing warmth and an agreeable atmosphere to draw in family and friends. If you feel depressed every time you enter this room, think why you are keeping it like this. Are you fearful of inviting people to share food with you? Now put down on paper what your special kitchen would be like.

STEP 10 SEASONINGS, SAUCES, AND SPICES

Check for:

✓ Rancid oils

✓ Old vinegars

✓ Stale spices and seasonings

✓ Sauces way past their best

✓ Stale cooking ingredients

Unfortunately, it can be very easy to keep cabinets full of ingredients that you use once or twice to make a special dish, and then they are rarely used again. And if all your seasonings and sauces are tightly packed in, those at the back can easily float past their use-by date without you realizing it. Spices in particular lose their pungency very quickly, so check on them frequently. Or, if you decant them into other

storage jars, note the last date to use them by. If you have kept too many old sauces and seasonings you lower the energy in this area, and symbolically say that you have lost your zest for life. So take the time now to plan a drastic clear-out before you are affected by the dull energy levels.

Get organized: First, take everything out of the cabinet and work systematically through all the products, throwing out any past their use-by date. Trash old spices or those that have lost their pungency. Throw out old flours or dried-up raisins. Clean up any mess; place spices in racks behind doors, and sauces and seasonings in separate sections so that you can find them easily.

Obvious benefits of clear-out

Cleaned-out cabinets with easy-to-find ingredients.

Emotional benefits of clear-out

An energy boost after removing all those decaying items.

Maintenance: Assess your cabinets every three months and immediately throw out what's gone stale or rancid.

A kitchen needs to nurture you. Keep the surfaces and floor clear, and the cabinets full of healthy, fresh products.

STEP 11 UNUSED APPLIANCES

Check for:

✓ Unwanted gifts at the back of cabinets

✓ Equipment that no longer works

✓ Special-offer buys such as waffle makers or juicers that you may have forgotten about

Impressive-looking machinery that sits on the counter gathering dust or hiding at the back of a cabinet is taking up precious kitchen space. Equipment that you don't use, or which is broken beyond repair, is not adding to the productivity of this very positive area in the home. Let it go, allowing room for machinery that is wanted.

Get organized: Sell unwanted juicers or bread makers, or give to a friend who wants one; repair broken appliances or junk them.

Obvious benefits of clear-out

Streamlined counter tops and tidier cabinets.

Emotional benefits of clear-out

Relief that you now only have loved and functioning kitchen appliances.

Maintenance: Repair malfunctioning equipment immediately, or you never will. Check again every three to six months.

STEP 12 REFRIGERATOR/ FREEZER

Check for:

✓ Frozen meat, fish, or vegetables beyond their use-by date

✓ Mystery bags of home-cooked food with freezer burn

✓ Abandoned condiment containers

✓ Products that have gone bad

✓ Rotting vegetables

A refrigerator/freezer represents the wealth and health of the family, so it should always be full of fresh and nourishing produce. Old, decaying, forgotten, or gunky foods represent a lack of concern for you or your family's welfare. Remove them immediately, and fill your refrigerator/freezer with food to entice the taste buds.

Get organized: Work through the refrigerator first. Eat up any leftovers within two days; remove any moldy food or suspect sauces, then clean out. Take any out-of-date meat, poultry, or vegetables from the freezer, wrap well, and throw away. Check for suspicious bags—dispense with anything unknown.

Obvious benefits of clear-out

A clean and bacteria-free refrigerator/freezer.

Emotional benefits of clear-out

A reassured feeling that you are safeguarding the family's health.

Maintenance: Have a quick check weekly; do a thorough investigation every two months.

Surround yourself with fresh vegetables to encourage good health in the family.

STEP 13 BROKEN AND DAMAGED CHINA

Check for:

✓ Chips and cracks on plates, bowls, and mugs, or cups

✓ Mismatched items

✓ Loose or broken handles on teapots and pitchers

If the dishware that you use daily for all your meals is damaged in any way, you are pulling down the positive energy of the kitchen area and not looking after yourself or your family. Chipped pieces can also be unhygienic and encourage bacteria. Clear the way for some bright, modern pottery.

Get organized: Check through all china carefully—hairline cracks can be easily missed; throw out mismatched, chipped, or badly damaged items. Use invisible glue on any loved possessions that can be saved.

Obvious benefits of clear-out

You are left with dishware that you are proud to use.

Emotional benefits of clear-out

A lack of irritation as you set the table.

Maintenance: Every time a serious chip appears, discard the piece. Check all china thoroughly every three months.

Regularly buy some new modern dishware to replace damaged items.

STEP 14 TRASH CAN AND UNUSED BAGS

Check for:

✔ Overflowing trash—cans, fish, and chicken bones, vegetable peel, milk cartons

✔ A less-than-fresh aroma

✔ Bottles, newspapers, and plastic containers around the trash

✔ Plastic or paper bags, stuffed by the refrigerator or in cabinets

What does trash say to you? Things that are finished with, scraps, decaying matter, or empty containers—basically it's all dead energy. There is nothing positive about an overflowing trash can—it is a dark space in your bright, sunny kitchen and needs controlling. Plastic bags always have a use, don't they? But if you keep hundreds, will you ever work through them all?

Get organized: Never overfill your trash; wrap left-over food well in newspaper; put newspapers, plastic, and glass bottles in your recycling bags or boxes. Re-employ a few plastic bags as liners for small pedal trash cans and ditch the rest. Keep a few for re-use.

Obvious benefits of clear-out
A more orderly, sweet-smelling kitchen.

Emotional benefits of clear-out
Your heart no longer sinks as you approach the trash area.

Maintenance: Empty the trash daily or every two days; keep only a few plastic or paper bags.

SUMMARY

Don't overestimate what you can do. Praise yourself for what you have managed, and appreciate how welcoming your kitchen is becoming.

It's important to update all your kitchen equipment regularly to lift the energy.

Aromatic sanctuary

STEP 15 KITCHEN REWARDS

Check for:

✓ Clearing out your refrigerator/freezer

✓ Tackling your store cabinets

✓ Re-organizing your kitchen china

✓ Discarding plastic or paper bags and tackling the trash

✓ Letting go of dusty appliances

If you haven't gotten as far with your de-junking as you would like, but have managed to reach at least two of the above goals, it's time for one or two encouraging treats to make your kitchen area more inspiring. Buy from the following list or make your own selection, but take your time and acquire only what you really want.

Clear-out treats

● Bright new cups or mugs

● A patterned fruit bowl—keep it full of fruit to symbolize abundance

● A coffee pot and fresh coffee to awaken your senses

● Pots of fresh, pungent herbs for the window ledge

● Storage jars to fill up with dried beans, rice, flour, or other ingredients to show a healthy household

● Pretty table mats and coasters to entice in dinner guests

STEP 16 YOUR WISH CARD

Before the end of your clear-out, select a wish card from your photocopies of the card on page 176. Write down your wish for your perfect kitchen or choose one of the following:

"I crave a streamlined, ordered kitchen."

"I want a kitchen that all my family comes together in."

"I yearn for a kitchen that I love to cook in."

"My perfect kitchen always smells wonderful."

"I want a desirable kitchen that is full of healthy produce."

"I seek a stimulating kitchen where I can create wonderful meals."

REAL-LIFE LETTING GO

Unhappy with all her discarded appliances, Sarah decided to take them to a garage sale along with some other unwanted possessions. The appliances in particular sold very quickly for the prices she wanted, and Sarah made enough to buy the elaborate juicer she had been wanting for months.

The Living Room Challenge

FOR A ROOM OF RELAXATION: 12 HOURS

Step 17—Complete the questionnaire (see pages 150–151) and study the living room

Step 18—Be ruthless with photographs

Step 19—Go through your bookshelves

Step 20—Look at your music collection

Step 21—Root through your magazine rack

Step 22—Check out your ornaments

Step 23—Decide about damaged furniture

Step 24—Appraise any inherited items

Steps 25 & 26—Your affirmation for success

STEP 17 MAKING ROOM FOR SOCIABILITY

Stand in your living room door. Are you shocked by the mess you are viewing? (Check your answers to the questionnaire).

● Do you hoard photographs?

● Are books, magazines, CDs, and DVDs scattered everywhere?

● Is the room overloaded with ornaments and decorations, and/or broken or inherited pieces?

This is your room for unwinding and entertaining, so it needs to have an uplifting, convivial ambience. Ask yourself why you are making this room so uninviting; are you pushing your friends away? Write down a description of your dream living room.

STEP 18 PHOTOGRAPHS AND ALBUMS

Check for:

✔ Out-of-focus shots

✔ Photographs of people you have forgotten or no longer see

✔ Too many pictures of ex-partners

Decluttering your collection can be tough because photos remind you of the good times—but having heaps of them lying around in piles keeps you too attached to your past. They connect you to the person you once were, rather than who you are now, and also to people who are no longer important to you.

Get organized: Throw out unwanted shots—weed out excess pictures of ex-partners, people you no longer see, or people you dislike. Store loved photos in albums or index systems rather than in piles or bundles. Frame some current pictures that you really like.

Obvious benefits of clear-out
Those irritating piles of photos have now gone from shelves or drawers.

Emotional benefits of clear-out
You cut the ties with people you don't need in your life.

Maintenance: Every six months, make it a priority to check through any new photos you've accumulated. If you take digital pictures, delete bad or unwanted shots as you go.

STEP 19 BOOKSHELVES

Check for:

✔ Vacation fiction

  ✔ Dusty, out-of-date reference books

  ✔ Fading classics, not read for years

  ✔ Old travel books

It may seem prestigious to have a massive collection of books, but if they are hardly ever read, you felt obliged to take them from a relative, or they are just gathering dust, again they just link you to your past and old ideals. You need to allow space to bring in some new, stimulating books or knowledge that will advance you.

Get organized: Sort through your books a shelf at a time. Take unwanted classics or paperbacks to thrift (charity) stores, hospitals, or libraries; get rid of old or out-of-date reference or travel books.

Keep the living room clutter-free and fill with plants and flowers for an embracing atmosphere.

Obvious benefits of clear-out
You see gaps in your once overloaded bookshelves.

Emotional benefits of clear-out
A feeling of letting go as you release books you no longer need.

Maintenance: Check every six months for paperbacks that have accumulated; audit any other titles yearly.

STEP 20 MUSIC COLLECTION

Check for:

✓ Discarded LPs

✓ Broken or warped cassettes

✓ Unwanted CDs

Your music collection should comprise albums that you really love and to which you regularly listen. As your body's energy changes over the years, so does your musical taste. You can hang on to some of your favorite old-time greats, but otherwise prepare yourself to let go of sentiment as you discard the music that you too have really outgrown.

Get organized: If you no longer have a record player, sell or give away all your old LPs and replace your favorites with the CD version; sort through, and throw out, any broken or poor-quality cassettes; pass on any CDs no longer played to friends, family, or thrift stores. Buy a new set of storage racks for your pared-down collection; store the albums you want to keep in alphabetical or category order for easy reference or access.

Obvious benefits of clear-out

You can find all the albums that you want to play, and your living room floor is clear of music-related clutter.

Emotional benefits of clear-out

After some initial sadness, you feel pleased that you now have only the music you really love and want to listen to.

Maintenance: Go through your collection yearly; if you buy albums regularly, investigate your music every six months.

STEP 21 MAGAZINE RACKS

Check for:

✓ Old holiday brochures

✓ Local magazines or newspapers from months ago

✓ Daily newspapers more than a week old

✓ Monthly magazines from a year back

✓ Any out-of-date catalogs

A bulging magazine rack will depress you every time you look at it—it creates a black "energy hole" in your living room. Do you cling to outdated fashion and designs catalogs, last season's vacation brochures, or newspapers? If so, ask yourself why you feel the need to hang onto past news, travel or events long gone. Are you afraid of living in the present?

Get organized: Keep only your current vacation brochures; cut out any interesting magazine or newspaper articles for filing. Hang on to current catalogs and let go of the rest. Bundle up and throw away everything you can't recycle.

Obvious benefits of clear-out

A magazine rack full of current reading material that stimulates you.

Emotional benefits of clear-out

You no longer have that nagging voice in your head telling you to sort this area out.

Maintenance: Go through the magazine rack each month to keep on top of the paper mound.

STEP 22 DAMAGED FURNITURE

Check for:

✓ Scratched tables

✓ Sofas with torn upholstery

✓ Dining chairs with wobbly legs

✓ Cushions with broken zippers

If your furniture looks neglected, what does that say about you and how you are leading your life? Any damaged items will pull down the overall energy flow in your home, so repair any pieces or junk them.

Get organized: Fill scratches and revarnish tables or get professional help; cover torn upholstery with a throw; re-glue or nail wobbly chairs or dump them. Throw out broken cushion covers and buy some colorful new ones.

Obvious benefits of clear-out

Repaired furniture and re-vamped furnishings add a new vibrancy to the room.

Emotional benefits of clear-out

Irritation at having damaged items goes, and you feel in control.

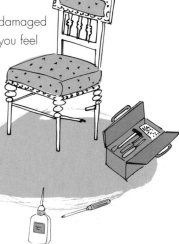

Maintenance:

Regularly look at furniture and furnishings; check thoroughly every three months.

Surround yourself with well-maintained furniture that you adore.

STEP 23 DECORATIONS

Check for:

✔ Unwanted gifts from friends and relations

✔ Vacation mementoes that no longer appeal

✔ Presents from past partners

Decorations and ornaments can be a prominent feature in the living room, so they need to give you good, positive vibes. Don't buy into the stock answer, "I have to keep it, it was a present from a relative." You have to love all the pieces you keep. If anything is affecting you negatively every time you look at it, such as a statue given to you by an ex-partner, it just has to go.

Get organized: Look at all ornaments with a critical eye and put to one side anything you dislike. Give away any item that brings up bad emotions about the person who gave it; some vacation mementoes soon lose their appeal, so pass them on.

Obvious benefits of clear-out
Space has appeared on your mantle and shelves.

Emotional benefits of clear-out
You are now surrounded by possessions that you truly love.

Maintenance: Review your decorations every six months, and regularly reposition them for a positive energy shift.

STEP 24 INHERITED ITEMS

Check for:

✔ Ceramic collections

✔ Dark, depressing furniture

✔ Pictures

✔ Clocks

✔ Medals and war memorabilia

✔ Relatives' knick-knacks

The emotion we attach to inherited possessions is amazing—we feel that person imbued in them, but preserving items from dead loved ones can create a mausoleum of mis-matched belongings. It is a tough one, but if the inherited pieces have no place in your decor, let them go. Remember they match the energies of the person who owned them, not yours.

Get organized: Keep only what you love—you will always remember that person; junk worthless mementoes. Sell collections, clocks, and furniture; make a remembrance collage of favorite old photos—discard the rest; keep or frame one or two medals or memorabilia, then sell or give the rest to a war museum.

Obvious benefits of clear-out
Your living room regains your chosen style.

Emotional benefits of clear-out
A wonderful feeling of letting go of the past.

Maintenance: Review every time belongings are passed on to you.

SUMMARY
Give yourself a pat on the back; your living room is now unrecognizable from the start of all your de-junking.

Sociable haven

STEP 25 LIVING ROOM REWARDS

Check for:

✓ Going through your photos

✓ Cutting down your book collection

✓ Disposing of unwanted music

✓ Trashing old magazines and newspapers

✓ Renovating furniture and furnishings

✓ Letting go of relatives' belongings

✓ Relinquishing some ornaments and decorations

How much have you done? If you have worked through at least four, ideally five, of the above goals, you are sorting out your clutter well and need a small treat to enhance your cleared-out living room. Choose from the following or make your own selection.

Clear-out treats

● A metal or wooden picture frame

● Healthy, round-leaf plants or flowers to encourage more growth

● Some incense, such as basil, jasmine, or patchouli to promote good feelings

● A new book or CD you have really wanted for some time

● Pebbles, or a glass, or ceramic ornament for some grounding energy

● A rug that will enhance your decor

STEP 26 YOUR WISH CARD

Before you finish your clear-out, take a wish card from your photocopies of the card on page 176. Write down a wish for your special living room from the following, or make one of your own.

"I want my living room to be warm and inviting."

"I need a living room that is calming and soothing."

"I long for my living room to be minimalist."

"My aim is to create a living room full of laughter and joy."

"I am making my living room a happy and pleasant family room."

"My dream living room is full of sociable people."

REAL-LIFE LETTING GO

Peter, a writer, loved his collection of books. But there were too many and they overcrowded his living room. He was reluctant to let go of some old paperbacks, but agreed he wanted space for new literature, and let them go. A few weeks later, he was offered a book deal from the same paperback publisher—he had let new opportunities come in.

The Bedroom Challenge

FOR A ROOM THAT CALMS: 7 HOURS

Step 27—Complete the questionnaire (see pages 150–151) and study the bedroom

Step 28—Look at the laundry

Step 29—Check out the bed

Step 30—Organize your clothes

Step 31—Cut down on your shoes

Step 32—Work through your cosmetics

Steps 33 & 34—Your affirmation for success

STEP 27 MAKING A ROOM FOR BLISSFUL SLEEP

Stand at your bedroom door. Do you feel your heart sink as you view the existing disorder? (Check your answers to the questionnaire.)

● Are there boxes bulging with clothes and is junk teetering on top of your closets?

● Is the space under your bed a secret hideout for broken or unwanted items, or discarded clothes?

● Do you find that it's difficult to find your favorite perfume because it is always buried under mounds of useless clutter?

This is your resting room, so it needs a calm, embracing atmosphere in order to encourage peaceful sleep. Ask yourself if the disorder here reflects some other confusion in your life. Now note down what your blissful bedroom would ideally be like.

STEP 28 THE LAUNDRY BASKET

Check for:

✔ Overflowing basket

✔ Discarded items

✔ Piles of clothes scattered around the room

A full laundry basket creates a stagnant space in the bedroom, slowing down energy flow. Clothes pick up the negative vibrations of a normal working day—traveling stress, office trauma, and any upsets with children. Random clothes piles create a gridlock of stale energy. If you don't get down to tackling the clutter mountains, your mood can be adversely affected by the mess.

Get organized: Start by moving the laundry basket into the bathroom or the utility room; hang up clothes each night—even when you get home late, never leave garments hanging over a chair or littering the floor.

Obvious benefits of clear-out

The room and floor look tidier and you can vacuum more easily.

Emotional benefits of clear-out

Your mood lightens as you are no longer annoyed by scattered or piled-up clothes around the room.

Maintenance: Wash clothes every couple of days to avoid any build-up.

STEP 29 THE BED

Check for:

✓ Broken equipment, dirty clothes, old shoes, junk under bed

✓ Age of mattress

✓ Age of bed linen and duvet covers

A bed can store people's energies. If you are in a new relationship but still sleep in the bed that a long-term partner shared, you have not broken the tie with that person. Junk under the bed can disturb sleep or take the zing out of your sex life.

Get organized: Buy a new bed or mattress, or at least new bed linen; clear out the area under the bed, throw away junk, and store what you keep in closets or drawers.

Obvious benefits of clear-out

You get a firm new bed or mattress to sleep on, or bright new bed linen.

Emotional benefits of clear-out

A new bed or linen means a new start. You will sleep better with your new partner.

Maintenance: Make one of the above changes when a long-term relationship ends.

STEP 30 CLOTHES

Check for:

✓ Clothes not worn for a year

✓ Out-of-shape, delicate, or itchy dresses

✓ Too tight or old-fashioned pants/jackets/shirts

Renew bed linen regularly and after a relationship ends.

✓ Outdated, jokey T-shirts

✓ Unworn business suits

✓ Worn coats/outdoor wear

✓ Torn clothes/broken zippers

Most of us wear only twenty percent of the clothes that we possess. Ask yourself why you are hanging onto things that no longer fit—why not buy clothes to flatter the current you? Clinging onto old items keeps you tied to your past image. Be ruthless: lay everything on the bed, and bring in a friend as an arbitrator to say what looks good on you.

Get organized: junk old, unworn, jokey, or disliked items; repair damaged clothes; buy multiple hangers; keep sweaters/T-shirts in clear plastic boxes; put work clothes at front and casual clothes at the back of the closet for easy access; place bags on large hooks.

Obvious benefits of clear-out

Everything fits in your wardrobe.

Emotional benefits of clear-out

You look good—and your self-esteem rockets.

Maintenance: Review every season; when you buy something new, get rid of something old.

Maintenance: Check seasonally, and remember if you buy a new pair of shoes, try to get rid of some old ones.

STEP 32 COSMETICS

Check for:

✔ Worn-down lipsticks, eyeliner pencils, ratty brushes

✔ Messy or dried-up foundations, moisturizers, lip gloss, mascara, nail polish

✔ Eyeshadows or blushers in unfashionable shades

Your make-up enhances the person you are today, not a few years ago, so it needs to be loved and up-to-date, and complement your clothes.

Get organized: Junk ancient messy make-up and brushes; throw away past season's eye shadows; keep only make-up used now; clean your make-up bag; store in clear plastic boxes.

Obvious benefits of clear-out

You can quickly find that favorite lipstick or pencil.

Emotional benefits of clear-out

You look and feel good.

Maintenance: Check every three months.

STEP 31 SHOES

Check for:

✔ Shoes/boots with broken heels

✔ Old-fashioned styles

✔ Too-tight shoes or heels

✔ Unworn impulse buys

Shoes keep us grounded in life, so they need to be supportive and comfortable so that we feel good about ourselves. If your closet is full of shoes that are broken, ones that torture you, or fashion-victim styles hardly worn, you are affecting your overall wellbeing.

Get organized: Pull shoes out, try them on, discard ones that are broken, uncomfortable, too high, or tight. Pass on to friends unworn or disliked styles. Store favorites neatly in pairs on racks.

Obvious benefits of clear-out

You can now see the bottom of your closet.

Emotional benefits of clear-out

You feel good wearing the shoes you love.

SUMMARY

Take a break—you have achieved a lot. Your bedroom is emerging as a much more inviting place to sleep.

Bedded bliss

STEP 33 BEDROOM REWARDS

Check for:

✔ Sorting out the laundry basket

✔ Reviewing your bed

✔ Re-organizing your clothes and shoes

✔ Paring down your cosmetics

If you are well on your way to achieving a minimalist bedroom, and have achieved at least two of the above goals, you are doing well. So choose a couple of the treats below, or make your own choice, but remember plants or water features are not suitable for the bedroom (in feng shui they are wonderful energizers, whereas in this room you need tranquility).

STEP 34 YOUR WISH CARD

Just before you finish your clear-out, take one of your photocopies of the card on page 176. Note down your wish for your special bedroom, or select one of the following.

"I need my bedroom to make me feel comforted and protected."

"I yearn to have restful and restorative sleep in my bedroom."

"I long for peace and tranquility in my bedroom."

"I crave my bedroom to be sensuous and loving."

"I am ready for a passionate, alluring bedroom."

Clear-out treats:

● A large lavender-scented candle

● An inspiring picture to hang opposite the bed

● A loving rose quartz crystal to go on your nightstand

● Cushions in a tactile material, such as velvet or satin

● An essential oil burner and some enticing ylang-ylang or rose essential oil

● A dreamcatcher to put over the bed to protect your dreams

If you choose the candle or aromatherapy oil burner, always extinguish the flame before sleep for safety reasons.

REAL-LIFE LETTING GO

Susan had been sleeping badly for a while and asked for my advice. On checking her bedroom, I found that her underbed area had become her dumping ground. It was littered with old shoes, discarded clothes, magazines, cat's toys, and a broken hairdryer. She threw the junk in the trash and vacuumed the area. She collapsed in bed that night, exhausted—and had her best night's sleep in many months.

The Child's Bedroom Challenge

FOR A ROOM OF REST AND STIMULATION: 5½ HOURS

Step 35—Complete the questionnaire (see pages 150–151) and assess your child's bedroom

Step 36—Look at the toy box

Step 37—Go through all clothes and shoes

Step 38—Sort out the underbed area

Step 39—Check for current sports equipment

Steps 40 & 41—Your affirmation for success

STEP 35 MAKING A ROOM FOR REST AND CREATIVITY

Study your child's room with a critical eye. Do you avoid going in there because of the existing chaos? (Check your answers to the questionnaire.)

● Are clothes scattered everywhere and falling out of the closets?

● Do you keep tripping over discarded toys?

● Have you spotted worn out racquets, bats, and balls threatening to break out from the closet—or unbelievable objects lurking under the bed?

A child's bedroom is a mixture of rest and play. It is here that he or she plays games, listens to music with friends, does homework, and finally drifts to sleep, so this room needs more of an uplifting atmosphere. If the room is overly cluttered, your child may be lethargic or sleep badly, or his/her school work may suffer. Write down how you think you can transform this room.

STEP 36 TOY BOX

Check for:

✔ Broken model cars, toy trucks, and trains

✔ Dolls with limbs missing; punctured balls, torn teddies or other soft toys

✔ Discarded toys that are linked to an old TV series

✔ Unread reading books or picture books, or those with ripped-out pages

Store only bed linen in your child's underbed area.

Young children have short attention spans. They happily play with a toy, lose interest or break it, and move on to something else. If their toy box is stuffed full of unused, broken, or dismembered toys, rather than loved ones, this creates a low-energy space.

Get organized: Pull out all the broken toys, torn books, and junk; give away character toys—other children may still like them. Take unwanted books to hospitals or libraries. Get more toy boxes, if needed, for loved toys—put the boxes on rollers so kids can easily pull out play items.

Obvious benefits of clear-out
Bringing some order to this messy box.
Emotional benefits of clear-out
Feelgood factor at giving toys to a deserving cause.

Maintenance: Check after every birthday and after Christmas each year.

STEP 37 CLOTHES AND SHOES

Check for:
✔ A trail of clothes around the room
✔ Outgrown dresses, pants, sweaters, baby clothes, shirts, T-shirts, and shoes
✔ Children's uncool clothing rejects
✔ Faded and frayed jackets and coats

Kids grow out of clothes fast, and if they are unworn they are cluttering up useful closet space. Clothes left on the floor carry the negative energies of the day, and need to be hung up or put in the laundry basket. Rejected or disliked clothing gives off bad vibrations in the closet.

Get organized: Install a laundry basket for dirty clothes; pass on outgrown or rejected clothes and shoes to friends' children or to charity. Dispense with worn-out, frayed clothing. Sort clothing into school and leisure wear; fit shoe racks and add shelving for sweaters, shirts, and T-shirts.

Obvious benefits of clear-out
Organized wardrobes and a tidier bedroom.
Emotional benefits of clear-out
You're happy that your child has a better environment for sleep and play.

Maintenance: Take a look every six months; every three months if your child is growing rapidly.

STEP 38 UNDER THE BED

Check for:

✓ Discarded pajamas, socks, screwed-up clothes, shoes, and sneakers

✓ Candy wrappers, half-eaten food, soda cans

✓ Abandoned games, half-finished puzzles, lost toys

✓ Computer games, disks, crayons, pencils, and scraps of paper

Losing sundry items under the bed is a common habit for both adults and children. But growing children can be more vulnerable to this stale pile of energy lingering beneath them when they are resting. It can cause erratic or disturbed sleep, and affect their concentration in everything they do. Make this a forbidden zone for junk.

Get organized: Throw out trash; wash dirty clothes; tidy away shoes. Store games and puzzles in a closet; put toys back in box. Place computer games and disks in neat racks and writing equipment in stationery holders. Clean well and keep nothing under the bed, or only some current clothes or linen in a pull-out drawer.

Obvious benefits of clear-out

A spotless area under the bed.

Emotional benefits of clear-out

You feel thankful that your child's room is now more conducive to sleep.

Maintenance: Patrol this area regularly—every two or three days.

STEP 39 SPORTS EQUIPMENT

Check for:

✓ Deflated soccer/rugby balls, old tennis balls, broken rackets, table tennis bats, baseball bats and mitts, abandoned skateboards, and frisbees

✓ Untouchable sneakers

Hoarding old unused sports equipment is just keeping your child linked to activities he or she no longer enjoys, or to an item he has long outgrown. Surround him with his current sporting loves.

Get organized: Throw away any damaged equipment; give rejects to friends or sports clubs. Store the remainder neatly in a designated section of the closet for easy retrieval.

Obvious benefits of clear-out

No more danger zones—abandoned equipment won't assault you as it falls out of the closet.

Emotional benefits of clear-out

A contented child with sports gear that he or she uses often.

Maintenance: Look at equipment yearly, or every six months for a sports fiend.

SUMMARY

Take a few deep breaths. You have tackled some tricky projects—especially if you've taken on an older child's bedroom. If you lost a few battles, think about convincing your child to clean in a different way.

A restful den

STEP 40 CHILD'S BEDROOM REWARDS

Check for:

✓ Sorting out the toy box

✓ Dejunking under the bed

✓ Streamlining sports equipment

✓ Updating clothes and shoes

This area is harder to declutter as it is more out of your control, but if you have achieved at least two of these goals, you deserve to buy one or two treats to make this tidier space more appealing. Select from the following, or choose your own treat.

Clear-out treats:

● A fabric laundry sack

● Brightly colored or transparent plastic toy boxes

● An amethyst crystal—put by the bed of an older child to balance their emotions

● A lamp for night-time reading

● A poster that your child loves

● A big cushion or beanbag for play and relaxation

STEP 41 YOUR WISH CARD

Before your clear-out ends, take a wish card from your photocopies of the card on page 176. Write down your own wish for your ordered child's bedroom, or put down one of the following:

"I desire my child's bedroom to be a restful sanctuary."

"I seek peace and order in my child's bedroom."

"I want my child to sleep contentedly in her bedroom."

"I yearn for my child to have a tidy bedroom."

"I long for my child's bedroom to be full of happiness."

"My child's bedroom will have a harmonious atmosphere."

REAL-LIFE LETTING GO

A client's daughter, Alison, was very attached to all her dolls but because she had so many, there wasn't room for all of them. After some persuading, she put her favorites to one side and allowed her mother to take the rest to a children's home. She felt a warm glow when her mother told her how happy the children were with their new playthings.

The Bathroom Challenge

FOR A ROOM THAT SOOTHES: 5¼ HOURS

Step 42—Complete the questionnaire (see pages 150–151) and assess the bathroom

Step 43—Inspect your towels and mats

Step 44—Get rid of those beauty samples

Step 45—Eliminate ex-partner's toiletries

Step 46—Streamline your medicine cabinet

Step 47—Take a look at your vacation treasures

Steps 48 & 49—Your affirmation for success

STEP 42 MAKING A ROOM FOR RECUPERATION

What do you feel about your bathroom when you step inside? Look around and detect any hotspots of disorder (check your answers to the questionnaire).

✔ Are too many towels or mats cluttering up the bathroom cabinet?

✔ Are your cabinets clogged up with old medicines, piles of beauty samples, or old toiletries?

✔ Have your vacation treasures set around the tub lost their sparkle?

Your bathroom can be a wonderful haven where you soak away the cares of the day. If it is an utter mess, think about why you are denying yourself the relaxation you deserve. Energy moves slowly in the bathroom (water is always draining here, making the room yin, or passive) so clutter here hinders the flow even further—and slows you up. Now write down how you see your ultimate bathroom.

STEP 43 TOWELS AND MATS

Check for:

✔ Stiff, torn, or frayed towels

✔ Garish embroidered or named gift towels

✔ Balding or faded mats

Towels should be fluffy and luxurious. If most of yours are in bad condition, you are denying yourself the comfort you deserve. Mats literally help you to keep your feet on the ground; if you're still using ones that are worn or threadbare, your standing in life is undermined.

Get organized: Weed out the worst towels or mats and dispose of them. Give away disliked gift towels—they may be to someone else's taste. Sort the rest by size with favorites and newest styles on top and mats beneath.

Obvious benefits of clear-out

You no longer have to use towels that scratch or have lost their fluffiness.

Emotional benefits of clear-out

You feel more nurtured and secure.

Maintenance: Look at your towels and mats every few months; visit the sales for towel bargains.

Store your bathroom products neatly in units or containers to let the energy flow freely.

STEP 44 BEAUTY SAMPLES

Check for:

✓ Mini toothpastes

✓ Conditioner, shampoo, and moisturizer sachets, face packs

✓ Tiny bath oils, creams, or body lotions

✓ Bottles of aftershave or perfume

Beauty samples come through the door all the time. They lodge themselves in the bathroom, and at first they are welcomed because they are free. If you love samples, you will probably use them in the first couple of weeks. Otherwise, they fester and eat up room in your cabinets—until you have a major clear-out.

Get organized: Samples are great, but just display prominently those you want as a reminder to use them—and lose the rest. Put some in your gym bag, or travel light with them on weekend getaways.

Obvious benefits of clear-out

More room for your favorite items.

Emotional benefits of clear-out

You feel in control once more.

Maintenance: Keep useful samples; trash others.

STEP 45 EX-PARTNER'S TOILETRIES

Check for:

✓ Bottles of aftershaves and perfume/cologne

✓ Toothpaste, toothbrush, mouthwash

✓ Disposable razors, shaving foam

✓ Deodorant, make-up remover, and moisturizer

✓ Shampoo and conditioner

If your bathroom is full of products your ex-partner left behind, you are creating a shrine to them and will find it even harder to let go of your love. Be easy on yourself; cut the ties on a day when you are strong.

Get organized: Search for any toiletries belonging to your ex and get them out of your home; clean the room thoroughly.

Obvious benefits of clear-out

More space for pampering products for you.

Emotional benefits of clear-out

That relationship is history—you're living in the now.

Maintenance: Be strong—vow to throw out or return all of your ex-partner's grooming products whenever a relationship ends.

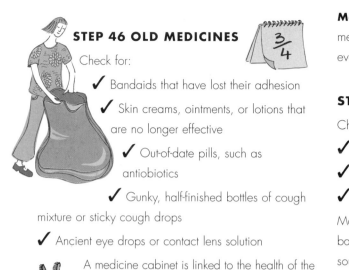

STEP 46 OLD MEDICINES

Check for:

✓ Bandaids that have lost their adhesion

✓ Skin creams, ointments, or lotions that are no longer effective

✓ Out-of-date pills, such as antiobiotics

✓ Gunky, half-finished bottles of cough mixture or sticky cough drops

✓ Ancient eye drops or contact lens solution

A medicine cabinet is linked to the health of the family and should be full of only current, prescribed remedies for ailments. Old medicines past their sell-by date encourage an atmosphere of ill health and can pull down the positive bathroom vibrations.

Get organized: Pick out anything that is out of date or unusable and throw away; return old antibiotics to a drug store/chemist. Get rid of half-finished grungy creams, ointments, and cough medicines. Re-plan your cabinet, drawers, or baskets to hold similar products together such as bandages and antiseptics.

Obvious benefits of clear-out

It's faster to find the medicine you're seeking.

Emotional benefits of clear-out

You feel better as all these old health products leave your home.

Maintenance: Your health is important, so don't keep medicine dregs. Check the validity of medications every three months.

STEP 47 VACATION TREASURES

Check for:

✓ Precious shells, pebbles, star fish

✓ Natural sponges

✓ Pieces of driftwood, feathers

Many of us love to decorate our bathrooms with natural vacation souvenirs, particularly shells. Rather than holding the memory of the good times in our heads we want a tangible possession. But vacations come and go, and so should these pieces when they are past their best.

Get organized: Get rid of dusty or rotting mementoes that now irritate you. Replace with current vacation finds.

Obvious benefits of clear-out

You have fewer items to clean.

Emotional benefits of clear-out

Releasing old attachments.

Maintenance: Renew your treasures regularly. Keep only what you love, and reappraise after each trip.

SUMMARY

Well that wasn't so bad, was it? You are well on the way to having the bathroom you want. Allocate more time to deal with any black spots.

Welcome retreat

STEP 48 BATHROOM REWARDS

Check for:

✓ Rationalizing beauty samples

✓ Being realistic about vacation treasures

✓ Updating your towels and mats

✓ Cutting back your medicinal supplies

✓ Trashing your ex-partner's bathroom goods

This is an important room to get right, but it takes time. If you have ticked off at least two goals above you are progressing well, and can allow yourself some treats to add to the ambience of this evolving room. Pick from the list below, or choose your own.

Clear-out treats

● Geranium or marjoram essential oil to calm you, or lime or lemon to invigorate (add eight drops to a warm bath)

● A big luxurious towel, just for you

● Several candles to go around the tub

● A patterned shower curtain that lifts your spirits and your inner energy

● A bath loofah for body brushing

● A spider plant or fern to increase the room's energy

If you choose candles, always safely extinguish them after your bath.

STEP 49 YOUR WISH CARD

Before the end of your clear-out, get one of your photocopied wish cards (see page 176) and write down your wish for your sublime bathroom, or choose one of the following.

"I want to make my bathroom a sensuous retreat."

"I long for a bathroom that honors my soul."

"I'd love a bathroom that fills me with tranquility."

"I want a bathroom full of inspiring scents."

"I am designing a bathroom that is my perfect retreat."

"I see my bathroom as my safe cocoon."

REAL-LIFE LETTING GO

A friend, Jane, always brought back some special shells from vacation for her bathroom collection. Although she always removed some before adding the new ones, she still spent more time cleaning the shells than her bathroom. When she asked for my help, I suggested she frame a collage of her favorite shells and discard the rest—a perfect solution to her dilemma.

The Attic Challenge

FOR A ROOM OF THE PAST: 8 HOURS

Step 50—Complete the questionnaire (see pages 150–151) and rate your attic

Step 51—Minimize your painting materials

Step 52—Let go of school memorabilia

Step 53—Part with love mementoes

Step 54—Sort through your Christmas decorations

Step 55—Rationalize your vacation box

Steps 56 & 57—Your affirmation for success

STEP 50 MAKING A ROOM FOR LETTING GO

Take a deep breath and go up into your attic. Can you easily get through the door, or is it jammed with boxes of junk? (Check your answers to the questionnaire.)

● Are there bursting bags of old festive decorations and dusty boxes of old love trinkets lying around?

● Do you trip over boxes from your school days?

● Are shelves where you store your vacation and decorating materials in complete disorder?

The attic is a wonderful place to store any possessions that are rarely used. But if it is so full of junk that you don't dare go in there, you are making it into a black hole full of slow, sticky energy that literally hangs over the household. Try and think why you feel you need to keep such an attachment to your past. Write down how you see this place with the clutter removed.

STEP 51 PAINTING MATERIALS

Check for:

✓ Dried-up paint and varnish tins

✓ Stiff brushes of all sizes

✓ Rollers that were once spongy or fluffy

✓ Old cleaning liquids and paint-spattered rags

✓ Sample paint pots and stencils

✓ Broken paint trays

Most of us are proud of how we have decorated our homes, but you have no need to hang on to paint "souvenirs" from a color scheme that changed years ago. Paint changes color or dries up, and as our energy changes so does our taste in color. Your favorite shade of five years ago will be different today.

Get organized: Dump dried-up paint and cans of varnish; please contact your local sanitation department for regulations regarding disposal of hazardous waste. Keep any fresh cans to touch up walls after minor bumps and scrapes. Lose dried-up brushes and disposable rollers (keep the handles), broken items, rags, liquids, and stencils. Group paints in room order, place brushes neatly in jars for easy access.

Obvious benefits of clear-out
You have an ordered decorating shelf or box.
Emotional benefits of clear-out
You let go of those old decorating memories.

Maintenance: Review every time you decorate another room.

STEP 52 SCHOOL MEMORABILIA

Check for:

✔ Exercise or school books

✔ Badges, medals, sashes, scarves, and hats

✔ Awards, diplomas, and degrees

✔ College projects and essays

✔ School reports

Hanging on to boxes of material from your school and college days will just keep you entrenched in your childhood Do you feel you have to justify what you have achieved, or were you happier in those days? You will always remember those times, but you are a different person now—so live in the present.

Get organized: Junk or recycle books, essays, and projects. Throw out long-forgotten awards; frame and display diplomas and degrees. Keep a small mementoes box with a few prize badges and other items for future generations.

Obvious benefits of clear-out

A clean, empty corner in the attic.

Emotional benefits of clear-out

Letting go of who you were, and celebrating who you are now.

Maintenance: This is a one-time clear-out, but ask children to do a sort out before they leave home.

STEP 53 LOVE MEMENTOES

Check for:

✔ Yellowing love letters

✔ Pressed or dried flowers

✔ Photos of old boyfriends or girlfriends

✔ Love gifts, cards, old pieces of jewelry

✔ Books of love poems, cuddly toys

This is an emotive area to deal with as everyone remembers their first love or a special partner. But hoarding too much from your past relationships stops you from releasing these people or enjoying a current relationship to the full. It can also prevent you from meeting a new lover.

Get organized: Re-read love letters, keep some special ones, and trash the rest. Put a few cherished cards, photos, or letters in a special love treasures box in an accessible place for when you feel sentimental.

Obvious benefits of clear-out

Extra attic space materializes.

Emotional benefits of clear-out

You put your past relationships behind you.

Maintenance: Check every year, and after a relationship ends.

An attic is ideal storage, but don't overcrowd it and store labeled boxes neatly.

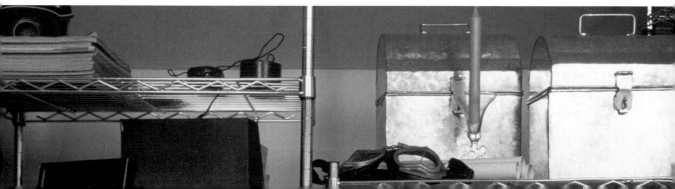

STEP 54 CHRISTMAS DECORATIONS

Check for:

✓ Broken lights, damaged artificial tree

✓ Tarnished tinsel, old streamers

✓ Discolored angels and santas

✓ Cracked or broken ornaments

✓ Flattened ornaments and moldy chocolate figures

With each Christmas, more decorations seem to get added to the groaning box in the attic, but how many old ones are hung up? This is a sentimental time, but don't preserve ancient decorations for the sake of it; it prevents you from bringing in new ones and fresh seasonal energy.

Get organized: Dig into the box. Keep that favorite angel, but discard broken or tatty decorations. Check lights, and ditch defective ones; replace bulbs on working strings. Add a section divider, placing rolled-up tinsel and streamers in one, ornaments in another, and so on.

Obvious benefits of clear-out

Usable decorations in a re-planned box.

Emotional benefits of clear-out

You let go of Christmas pasts.

Maintenance: Check yearly in early December.

STEP 55 VACATION BOX

Check for:

✓ Last year's sun lotions and creams

✓ Broken or perished snorkels, masks, and fins

✓ Out-of-date insect repellent, half-empty first-aid kit

✓ Faded caps, torn sarongs, worn-out beach bags, unused travel games

✓ Travel hairdryer and plugs that don't work

After a vacation, don't throw your regular vacation gear back in its box—make sure it's worth keeping. Hoarding too much vacation junk can deplete the enjoyment of your next trip, so evaluate it before you go.

Get organized: Discard sunscreen lotions more than a year old—their protective properties are lost. Throw out worn-out travel goods; mend or junk broken items; give away games to other travelers; check the dates of first-aid kit contents; replace missing medicines.

Obvious benefits of clear-out

You find what you want with ease.

Emotional benefits of clear-out

You plan your next trip with a light heart.

Maintenance: Assess twice a year and see what useless goods have crept in.

SUMMARY

Well done—it is hard work to declutter here, but see how space is now emerging in this once overcrowded room.

Re-planned store room

STEP 56 ATTIC TREATS

Check for:

✓ Streamlining your decorating materials

✓ Letting go of your school memories

✓ Dealing with those love tokens

✓ Bringing some order to your vacation goods

✓ Saying goodbye to Christmas rejects

If you have had a bit of a struggle but still managed to do at least two of the above, you can allow yourself some treats to make your attic a more appealing space. Choose your own useful items, or select from the list below.

Clear-out treats

● Easy-to-fix shelving

● A bulkhead light fitting to bring some light energy into this dingy room

● Hardwearing crates on wheels so that you can move them around

● Attractive labels so that you can find everything you store

● Inexpensive units with small drawers for those small accessories you need to keep

STEP 57 YOUR WISH CARD

Before you finish clearing out, take one of your photocopies of the card on page 176. Write down your own wish for your ideal attic, or choose one of the following:

"I aim to have an attic that has plenty of good storage."

"I'd like my attic to be full of ordered boxes and neat shelving."

"I want an attic that is a pleasure to go in."

"I desire an attic space with very little stored in it."

"I long for an attic with very few possessions from my past."

"I need an attic with easy access."

REAL-LIFE LETTING GO

A client, Chris, needed a lot of encouragement to junk the twenty years' worth of credit card statements stored in his attic. Although he realized that they were irrelevant to his life today and tied him to his younger self, long gone, he was using them to remember happy events from years gone by. When he saw how his nostalgia had really been overshadowing his present life, he found it easier to let go of those slips of paper.

The Home Office Challenge

FOR A ROOM OF CREATIVITY: 10½ HOURS

Step 58—Complete the questionnaire (see pages 162–163) and study the home office

Step 59—Inspect office equipment

Step 60—Rake through filing cabinets (personal)

Step 61—Check out filing cabinets (financial)

Step 62—Look at the pinboard

Step 63—Sort out desk correspondence

Step 64—Appraise personal organizer/Palm pilot

Step 65—Delete emails/unwanted computer files

Steps 66 & 67—Your affirmation for success

STEP 58 MAKING A ROOM OF INSPIRATION

Have a look inside your office—the place where you spend all your days if you are self-employed. Does it fill you with dread every time you enter, because of the mess and unfinished tasks that exist there.

● Have you got equipment lying around that doesn't work?

● Are your filing cabinets and stationery units full of things you don't need?

● Do you have contact names, addresses, and correspondence that date back a long time?

● Is your computer clogged up with old emails, programs, and files?

A home office is where you handle the home's finances and correspondence, push forward new projects, and create future proposals. If there is clutter scattered all around you, you will work in a confused, disjointed way and not achieve the tasks you set yourself. Write down how you see your model working office.

STEP 59 OFFICE MACHINERY

Check for:

✓ Malfunctioning printers, photocopiers, and fax machines

✓ Old computers, or ones that keep crashing

✓ Crackly or noisy phones, faulty pocket recorders

If you are surrounded by machinery that is broken or not working properly in your office, it affects the vibrancy of the room's energy and can disrupt your communication with your clients. It also shows a lack of concern for how you run your business.

Get organized: Call in professionals to fix machines that are not working well; dispose of those that are broken, old, or used. Get faults fixed on phones, or replace if unrepairable.

Obvious benefits of clear-out
A better functioning office with higher energy levels.
Emotional benefits of clear-out
A feeling of satisfaction that you communicate properly with the outside world.

Maintenance: Have all major equipment serviced yearly; get problems fixed as soon as they occur.

STEP 60 FILING CABINETS (PERSONAL)

Check for:

✓ Papers from failed courses

✓ Divorce papers from years ago

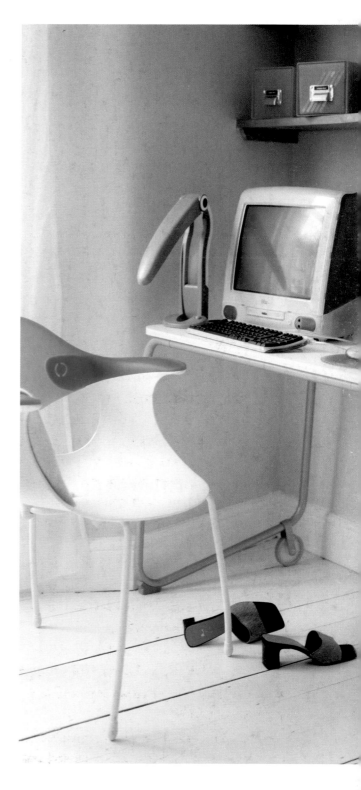

✓ Hospital letters concerning past illnesses

✓ Clippings files of things you plan to do

✓ Vacation bookings dating back years

✓ Old society memberships

Personal files can easily fill up with excessive paperwork that soon dates, so they need to be patroled regularly. Also if you are holding on to files that dealt with former break-ups, illnesses, or things not completed or done, you are linking into unnecessary negativity from your past.

Get organized: Keep current legal papers, bin old hospital and vacation correspondence, dated course material, and lapsed membership details. Label files clearly; discard clippings more than a year old; retain those that are still useful; put current ones in plastic sleeves in a ring binder file.

Obvious benefits of clear-out

Order is restored to your bulging cabinet.

Emotional benefits of clear-out

You have a positive energy surge as old papers are released.

Maintenance: Have a major clear-out yearly; do a quick check every three months.

Make sure that your desk area is neat and tidy so that you work in a positive way.

STEP 61 FILING CABINETS (FINANCIAL)

Check for:

✓ Papers relating to out-of-date loans

✓ Out-of-date insurances, accountant's correspondence, savings plans

✓ Mortgage papers from past properties

✓ Old letters to bank or pension companies, overdrawn bank statements, and credit card bills

Your office needs a vibrant atmosphere to deal with your home affairs or work successfully on business projects. If your financial filing cabinet is cluttered up with papers that relate to borrowings, defunct savings, or loans from years back, you are not encouraging a healthy flow of monies into your bank account.

Get organized: Throw away paperwork for paid-up loans and closed savings accounts. Retain important financial correspondence relating to the last few years; get rid of anything unimportant. If you are self-employed, keep the required bank statements for the necessary years, discard the remainder plus irrelevant credit card statements.

Obvious benefits of clear-out
You find all your financial papers quickly.
Emotional benefits of clear-out
The bond with old financial worries is broken.

Maintenance: Be strict with what you retain; purge files every six months and after financial changes.

STEP 62 PINBOARD

Check for:

✓ Notes more than six months old

✓ Old change-of-address cards, unused business cards

✓ Scribbled phone numbers, outdated contacts, and restaurant cards, old take-out menus

✓ Yellowing timetable for health club classes, last year's calendar

Pinboards are great places to store contact numbers for the people or places whom you regularly call. But if the board is clogged up with numerous old pieces of paper and unknown cards, you are creating an area of confusion and frustration where you never find what you want.

Get organized: Remove everything from the board methodically. Sort into useful and out-of-date piles, and discard the latter. Pin current cards and menus back on the board; transfer scrawled phone numbers to your organizer. Add this year's calendar and your latest gym timetable.

Obvious benefits of clear-out
You can find the contact number you want.
Emotional benefits of clear-out
A clearer head as another area of confusion disappears.

Maintenance: Every two months, remove any debris that has accumulated on the board.

STEP 63 DESK CORRESPONDENCE

Check for:

✔ Piles of letters over a week old

✔ Unpaid bills and invoices

✔ Unanswered invitations

✔ Piles of marketing and press information

✔ Unread reports, contracts

Your desk is the linchpin of your office. It is from here that you plan projects, give birth to new ideas, and run your day-to-day affairs. Submerging it in a mound of unanswered paperwork will make you feel disorientated and you'll work in a haphazard, distracted way.

Get organized: Be strict with yourself. Reply to letters and invitations the same day or email a reply, then file; have an invoice folder and set a weekly/monthly date to pay invoices; read promotional material, file anything useful, or throw out. Read reports and contracts, then pass them on or keep for reference.

Obvious benefits of clear-out

You have desk space to work on tasks in hand.

Emotional benefits of clear-out

Your mind clears and your concentration improves.

Maintenance: Work on having an empty desk each night; check weekly if the paper mountain starts to grow again.

STEP 64 PERSONAL ORGANIZERS

Check for:

✓ Contact details for people you no longer see

✓ Scraps of paper with phone numbers

✓ Post-its stuck on organizer

✓ Travel tickets, old notes, crumpled business cards, or shopping lists stuck inside

An organizer should live up to its name and help, rather than hinder, your daily working life. It is your ready access to your business and personal contacts, and needs to be full of positive people who will aid your working life. If it is bulging with trivia, or packed with old associates or disliked people, you are affecting your chances of business success.

Get organized: Remove extraneous pieces of paper and tickets, transfer useful information or numbers from notes and Post-its; carefully flick through crossing out unwanted details; re-write altered pages. Do the same with a Palm pilot, electronically deleting what is not needed.

Obvious benefits of clear-out

An organizer that you can easily open where you can find the number you need.

Emotional benefits of clear-out

You feel back in control, and can take on the world.

Maintenance: Review every six months. As contacts change, delete them. Check for accumulating junk every month.

STEP 65 EMAILS AND COMPUTER FILES

Check for:

✓ Unanswered emails

✓ Fifty-plus emails still in inbox

✓ Old project or correspondence files

✓ Unused programs

A computer is a valuable working tool, and like other equipment in your office, can have information overload. Seventy percent of a computer's hard disk should be kept free for it to work fast and efficiently. So if you don't archive material regularly you, like your computer, will work more slowly and not progress with important projects or new ideas.

Get organized: Answer emails daily then delete, print out, or file in folders on your hard disk. Delete older, irrelevant files or archive onto back-up disks. Remove unused programs, or get professional help.

Obvious benefits of clear-out

An efficient computer that is less prone to "crashing" or "freezing."

Emotional benefits of clear-out

You feel a surge of creativity, and notice that you are achieving much more than usual.

Maintenance: Stay on top of your emails; regularly clear out files every three months. Have a professional overhaul on your computer every year.

SUMMARY

Well done—the atmosphere is now much more conducive to successful working.

Inspiring domain

STEP 66

Check for:

✓ Working office equipment

✓ Attacking all mail

✓ Pruning material in filing cabinets

✓ Renewing your pinboard

✓ De-junking old contacts

✓ Spring-cleaning your computer

An office is one of the worst areas for clutter, so don't be surprised if it is taking time to clear. If you have managed at least three—ideally four—of the above goals, you can get some treats to make your office a better place. Buy from the list below, or invent your own.

Clear-out treats

● A peace lily or golden pothos plant to soak up computer emissions

● Transparent disk box, or stacking plastic boxes for stationery items

● An ergonomic, high-backed office chair for back support

● Packs of colored files

● A modern desk lamp to light your way

● A fan to keep the office cool through the summer

STEP 67 YOUR WISH CARD

Near the end of your clear-out, choose a photocopy of the card on page 176. Write down your wish for your perfect office, or select from the following.

"I want an office that enhances my creativity."

"My dream office promotes my success."

"I desire a practical office space."

"I yearn for an office full of inspirational energy."

"I crave an office that helps me achieve my goals."

"I need an office that encourages my financial security."

REAL-LIFE LETTING GO

I could hardly enter Barbara's home office. Household items were beating a path out of the closets and office paperwork was piled up everywhere—from the floor to the edges of her desk, where she could barely locate the phone. Together we removed a lot of useless clutter, and she did more on her own. A few weeks later she rang me to say how different she felt—she had more energy, and had acquired three new clients.

The Front Garden Challenge

STEP 68 MAKING A DESIRABLE SPACE

Stand outside your home and look toward your front space from the path. Do you really feel drawn to enter? Or do you feel upset because the whole area is so untidy and overgrown? (Check

your answers to the questionnaire.)

● Are there overflowing trash cans and broken pots everywhere?

● Have your boundaries and path become run down or do they need a good de-junking?

● Do you fight with shrubs or creepy-crawlies to get to your front door?

If you are finding your front area unappealing, or have to battle to your front door, muse about how visitors must feel. The front of your home is the first impression that you give to people, so it needs to be attractive

and appealing. If it is an utter mess, are you trying to stop people coming in? Put down on paper how you would like to change this space.

Maintenance: Clean out moss and weeds monthly. See if any renovation is necessary in the fall.

STEP 69 DAMAGED FENCES AND WALLS

Check for:

✔ Fence falling down or broken sections

✔ Frost-damaged, cracked, peeling, or broken wall

A wall or fence protects your property, giving you a safe boundary. But if it is in disrepair or falling down, ask yourself why you are subliminally removing boundaries with your neighbors and letting them intrude upon your personal space.

Get organized: Restore missing fence panels or sections, and paint or stain. Replace broken bricks or stones, and fill cracks, or have your wall rebuilt.

Obvious benefits of clear-out
Your territory is now clearly demarcated.
Emotional benefits of clear-out
Your personal boundaries are back in place, you feel secure once more.

Maintenance: Search for any signs of decay every six months.

STEP 70 DILAPIDATED GATE

Check for:

- ✔ A gate falling off its hinges
- ✔ Peeling or rusting paintwork, rotting wood on gate and posts
- ✔ Weeds creeping up the posts and hinges
- ✔ Creaking, rusty hinges

Make your front gate and path as appealing as possible to draw people in.

A gate is the first way in to your home, so if it is neglected or falling apart, what impression do you think people have of your home and the way you live? It is as though you are trying to bar entrance to your sanctuary, so get it fixed and let visitors flow in once more.

Get organized: Repair the existing gate and posts or buy new ones, if they are wooden and rotted. Rub down old paintwork with glasspaper, and re-paint or varnish for protection.

Obvious benefits of clear-out

A smart gate that operates smoothly.

Emotional benefits of clear-out

A feeling of opening yourself up to new opportunities.

Maintenance: Check your gate each spring to see if anything needs oiling or renewing.

STEP 71 BUILDERS' RUBBLE

Check for:

✔ Old bags of sand, cement, bricks

✔ Removed fittings such as baths and toilets

✔ Pieces of wood, plasterboard, old carpet, or flooring

If your home is being renovated, there will be materials stored outside temporarily. But if the work is finished, and messy rubble piles are left behind, it makes a dead energy space that needs removing before family life is affected.

Get organized: The rubble is the builders' responsibility, so ask them to come back and remove it. Alternatively, take what you can to the dump, or pay someone to remove it.

Obvious benefits of clear-out

You have reclaimed your space.

Emotional benefits of clear-out

You are not annoyed approaching your home.

Maintenance: Make sure that builders remove any debris before they finish improvement works.

STEP 72 TRASH CANS

Check for:

✓ Trash can positioned near the front door or outside the home

✓ Decaying matter scattered around trash can

✓ Too much in trash cans

A trash can full of dirty containers and decaying matter is a major area of negative energy outside your home, so it should be positioned as far away from your front door as possible. If it is too close, it will blight the vibrancy of the chi that enters your home through the front door.

Get organized: Never place your trash can in direct line with your front door—always put it to one side. Clean up stray waste, bag up well to prevent odors escaping; try to keep it well away from scavenging animals.

Obvious benefits of clear-out

You don't trip over the trash can as you head toward your door.

Emotional benefits of clear-out

You notice a better atmosphere in your hall.

Maintenance: Be vigilant about clearing up stray garbage around the trash can. If you get too many bags days before it is going to be collected, take them to the waste center yourself.

STEP 73 OVERGROWN SHRUBS AND TREES

Check for:

✓ Trees overhanging path, taking over house

✓ Tall bush at front blocking light

✓ Overgrown creeper around door

✓ Prickly bushes or parasitical weeds by path

Overgrown shrubbery in your front area can make it gloomy and dark. If people are also pushing past branches or prickly bushes just to get to your door, many won't bother.

Get organized: Hack back overgrown shrubbery, prickly bushes, and strangling weeds, or get professional help to lighten the area and expose the pathway.

Obvious benefits of clear-out

A front space that people want to enter.

Emotional benefits of clear-out

A feeling of being opened up to the world again.

Maintenance: Do major work here each season; trim regularly each month.

STEP 74 UNKEMPT PATH

Check for:

✔ Broken or
uneven paving stones or slabs

✔ Tall weeds or moss

✔ Overgrown plants

A path is a conduit for positive chi to enter your home. If you let it become overgrown with weeds or plants, or fall into general disrepair, you are disrupting this energy path and creating an unsettled, changeable atmosphere.

Get organized: Replace damaged stones or slabs; remove weeds or moss, and generally clean; cut back overgrown plants. Chi should move in spirals to the door, so try to lay a path in this pattern or add some pots or plants at different intervals to break up the straight energy flow.

Obvious benefits of clear-out

You don't have to watch where to walk.

Emotional benefits of clear-out

A more positive attitude as you approach your home.

Maintenance: Clean out moss and weeds monthly. See if any renovation is necessary in the fall.

Regularly dead-head flowers, cut back shrubs, and cut the grass for an ordered garden.

STEP 75 ROTTING FLOWERPOTS

Check for:

✓ Pots with frost damage

✓ Cracks, chips, or moss on pots

✓ Dead plants, old compost in pots

Pots full of scented flowers around your front door or lining an apartment balcony draw admiring looks from all, and they make an area of positive energy and growth. But pots that are full of weeds or dead plants have an air of neglect, introducing a negative energy flow that affects everyone.

Get organized: Throw out pots beyond repair; clean up mossy ones, and buy some new terra-cotta ones. Add new compost and healthy, seasonal flowering plants. Place one on each side of front door to attract in visitors.

Obvious benefits of clear-out
A tidier, more appealing space.

Emotional benefits of clear-out
You heart lifts looking at beautiful, healthy flowers.

Maintenance: Check the condition of pots every season; replace plants, renew compost.

STEP 76 GARDEN PESTS

Check for:

✓ Flies or other pests

✓ Slugs, snails, ants, and caterpillars

If you walk through your garden and everywhere you look you see pests eating away at your flowers and vegetables, you have a big problem to resolve. Apart from the bad effect on all your plants, if the pests are in control, symbolically you are allowing all the goodness to be sucked out of your life.

Get organized: Try to use organic methods to get bugs under control as insecticides will pollute the environment. Remove slugs and snails with animal-friendly pellets; cut back badly nibbled plants.

Physical benefits of clear-out
Healthier-looking plants and vegetables.

Emotional benefits of clear-out
More energy and a feeling of balance as your plants get back to normal.

Maintenance: Examine weekly in spring and summer.

SUMMARY

Don't be disheartened if you haven't managed everything. You have made a good start and your front space is starting to have an appealing atmosphere.

Glorious flowering pots add vibrancy and structure to your balcony or yard.

Inspiring space

STEP 77 FRONT YARD/GARDEN REWARDS

Check for:

✓ Sorting out your flowerpots

✓ Hacking back overgrown shrubbery

✓ Repairing gates and fences

✓ Renewing the path to your door

✓ Clearing away builders' rubbish

✓ Tidying up your trash cans

✓ Getting rid of excessive bugs

Are you exhausted? Clearing out the garden can be hard work, but if you have gotten through at least four, hopefully five, of the above goals, your front area is well on its way to being approachable once more, and you deserve a few treats. Choose from the list below, or invent your own.

Clear-out treats:

● A bird table

● A five-rod wind chime for the front door to slow down incoming chi

● Big terra-cotta or ceramic pots for welcoming flowers for your entrance

● Hanging baskets

● Small water fountain (on left-hand side as you look out of your front door) to boost chi flow

● Trellis fencing to grow scented climbers

STEP 78 YOUR WISH CARD

Toward the end of your clear-out, pick one of your photocopies of the card on page 176. Note down your wish for your special front space from the following, or think of one of your own.

"I want a front area that people are drawn to."

"I dream of a front space with alluring scents."

"I yearn for the front of my home to have structure and order."

"I seek a front space with a charming ambience."

"I desire a front area that I long to return home to."

"My perfect front space is full of flowering shrubs."

REAL-LIFE LETTING GO

Roger had become reclusive after his previous relationship ended. As I fought my way past all the shrubs to his front door, I realized how he was subconsciously pushing people away. I told him that he needed to clear this area and make it more inviting. He followed my advice and, about a month later, he called to say that his social life was improving and he had invited a woman to dinner that night.

The Back Garden Challenge

FOR A VERDANT RETREAT: 13½ HOURS

Step 79—Complete the questionnaire (see pages 166–167) and pace around your backyard or garden

Step 80—Check for any blocked drains

Step 81—Search for dying flowers

Step 82—Delve in the pond

Step 83—Sort out any dead tree stumps

Step 84—Work on the overcrowded shed

Step 85—Renovate garden furniture

Step 86—Look at any garden statues

Steps 87 & 88—Your affirmation for success

STEP 79 MAKING A SPECIAL RETREAT

Stand at your back door and note your impressions of your back space. Does it draw you to go and sit in it? Or is it simply just a chaotic mess? (Check back to your answers to the questionnaire.)

● Are you accosted by the unpleasant odor of blocked drains, a stagnant pond, and a dying tree?

● Can you never find your faded garden furniture in your overcrowded shed?

● Do you keep meaning to cut back old flowers and update any statues you own?

The backyard or back garden is your place for growing plants, relaxation, and entertaining. If you are surrounded by junk and decaying items, the atmosphere will reflect this and you will not want to linger here. Write down the ways in which you can transform this space.

STEP 80 BLOCKED DRAINS

Check for:

✓ Overflowing drain

✓ Leaves, twigs, garden debris

✓ Unpleasant smell

Keeping everything working efficiently in your home and backyard is important, because any problems create an energy block that can slow down the functioning of your household. Blocked drains prevent the natural water draining process, producing stale, bad-smelling water, so they need to be sorted out straight away.

Get organized: Clear out all the debris in the drain and add some cleansing fluid. If it is still not working well, call out some professionals.

Obvious benefits of clear-out

The blockage is removed and water flows away freely once more.

Emotional benefits of clear-out

As the chi movement improves, so does your family interaction.

Maintenance: Keep a vigilant eye on drains. If you notice any flooding out back, check immediately. Clean out regularly, particularly in the fall when there are a lot of leaves around.

STEP 81 DYING FLOWERS

Check for:

✓ Plants attacked by bugs, fungal, or viral disease

✓ Flowers past their best

Like your home, your yard or garden needs to be a vibrant area, full of healthy, growing plants, particularly the flowering varieties. If you look out of your back door and see a mass of wilted or dying flowers, doesn't the low energy there make you feel depressed? Keep your garden looking good and your inner chi stays high.

Get organized: Dead-head any old flowers to allow for new flowering; cut back any plants under attack from bugs. Replace dead plants with seasonal flowering varieties.

Obvious benefits of clear-out

A tidy backyard or garden full of healthy plants.

Emotional benefits of clear-out

Your spirits rise looking at the glorious flowers you have planted.

Maintenance: Regularly dead-head during the summer; review plants each spring and fall.

Look after all your garden furniture, so that you can set it out each year for summer dining on your patio.

STEP 82 THE POND

Check for:

✓ Stagnant, murky water, floating leaves

✓ Sick fish

✓ Dying plants, slimy residue

A pond can be a vital part of a garden, especially if it contains fish, as they help to keep the water moving, encouraging the general circulation of positive energy. But if has been neglected, it becomes a liability as the stagnant water can have a detrimental effect on the family's finances.

Get organized: Remove stagnant water and clean out the pond, getting rid of dead plants and sick fish. Fill with clean water and install a small pump to keep the water flowing and encourage good chi. Add a filter to keep the water fresh; restock with rocks, plants, water lilies, and fish—in feng shui, nine fish are considered auspicious.

Obvious benefits of clear-out

A clean, vibrant pond that is a joy to look at.

Emotional benefits of clear-out

A black cloud lifts from you as you eliminate the negativity that existed here.

Maintenance: Do minor cleaning tasks weekly. Check filter and pump following manufacturer's instructions. Have a major clear-out once a year.

STEP 83 DEAD TREE STUMPS

Check for:

✓ Rotting stump from felled tree

✓ Dying tree

An old tree stump is one of the worst things to have in your back space. It emits negative, dead energy, which floods out into the rest of the garden; ultimately it may affect the healthy atmosphere of your home.

Get organized: Have the stump dug out completely as soon as possible. Or, place a large chunk of clear quartz on it to counteract the decay. Call in a tree surgeon for advice on dying or unhealthy trees.

Obvious benefits of clear-out

This dying eyesore is removed from sight.

Emotional benefits of clear-out

The lethargy that has become part of your life finally lifts.

Maintenance: Check your trees each season. At any sign of decay, seek professional advice.

STEP 84 OVERCROWDED SHED OR OUTBUILDING

Check for:

✓ Rusting garden tools, perished hoses, watering cans, paddling pools

✓ Broken garden chairs, tables, or umbrellas

✓ Old fertilizer, plant liquids, seeds, pots

✓ Decrepid bicycles, sports equipment

✓ Useless gadgets and junk, broken barbecue set and mower.

If you can't get the door open to your shed, it has probably become your next junking ground as your attic is full. Don't think that just because it is outside it won't affect you—your shed is still draining your home's overall energy. A shed is a good storage area for garden accessories and outdoor equipment in regular use, so make sure that this is what it contains.

Get organized: Trash any junk, old plant foods, and seeds, and equipment that is beyond repair. Put everything that you want to keep on the lawn or deck, then clean the shed well. Salvage and oil any rusty tools worth keeping. Get as much off the shed floor as possible by adding more shelves for items such as fertilizers and flower food; hang working tools and equipment on hooks or on peg rails. Keep any garden chairs and barbecue equipment stored by the door for easy access; padlock to keep kids out.

Obvious benefits of clear-out

You now have a well-ordered storage space.

Emotional benefits of clear-out

There is no longer a sense of dread as you enter your shed.

Maintenance: Clutter creeps back. Clear out seasonally—every three months.

Use the warm, soft light of candles to illuminate the way to your yard's dining space.

STEP 85 GARDEN FURNITURE

Check for:

✓ Peeling paint, faded wood color

✓ Ripped or stained cushions, torn fabric

✓ Broken or cracked struts or supports

Garden furniture is dragged out in the summer months to take advantage of entertaining on sunny days, and then it is often left to languish for the rest of the year. If you neglect it, allowing chairs and tables to fall into disrepair, you are affecting the feelings of support and comfort needed in your life.

Get organized: Check over furniture. Discard any ancient pieces and replace; repair broken supports and replace fabric or cushions, if worthwhile. Rub down painted furniture with glasspaper and re-paint; re-stain colored woods.

Obvious benefits of clear-out

Your furniture works properly and looks like new.

Emotional benefits of clear-out

You no longer feel ashamed to bring out your garden furniture.

Maintenance: Clean well before storing each fall; check for repairs and any necessary replacements each spring.

STEP 86 GARDEN STATUES

Check for:

✓ Frightening gargoyles, demons, or imps

✓ Figures with broken arms or heads

✓ Overgrown or neglected statues

Your backyard or back garden should be a tranquil, relaxing place, so be careful what statuary you place there. Scary statues can generate a bad atmosphere, while broken male or female figures can symbolically encourage a health problem for a family member.

Get organized: Get rid of frightening or broken statues; scrub neglected ones. Display entwined or cupid statues to boost a relationship. Place a crane statue at the front and a tortoise at the back of the garden for harmony and a long life.

Obvious benefits of clear-out

You garden looks less of a junk yard.

Emotional benefits of clear-out

The balanced ambience means you feel calmer.

Maintenance: Clean well twice a year, and more frequently after inclement weather.

SUMMARY

Congratulate yourself; you have made a good start. Your backyard is really taking shape, so take some time out to sit there and admire it.

Glorious refuge

STEP 87 BACKYARD/GARDEN REWARDS

Check for:

✓ Purging your pond

✓ Removing decaying tree stumps

✓ Tackling your heaving shed

✓ Revamping your garden furniture

✓ Cutting back any wilting flowers

✓ Clearing any blocked drains

Do you feel pleased with yourself? Even if you have not tackled all the garden tasks you wanted, if you have managed at least three of the above goals, you can allow yourself a few treats. Select from the list below, or invent your own.

Clear-out treats

● A garden umbrella for shade and protection

● Garden lanterns or flares for summer entertaining

● A sun lounger to help you re-energize

● A hammock

● A barbecue or new accessories

● Strings of lights to illuminate the pathways

STEP 88 YOUR WISH CARD

As you finish your clear-out, draw a card from your photocopies of the card on page 176. Write your wish for your idyllic back garden space from the following, or invent your own.

"I want my backyard (garden) to be an oasis of calm."

"I desire a backyard that is a magical haven."

"I see my back garden space as a Mediterranean paradise."

"I crave a backyard full of friends and laughter."

"I seek a back area where I can meditate and escape the world."

"My exquisite backyard has a hidden patio for romantic dining."

REAL-LIFE LETTING GO

Julie could not understand why her friends never seem to want to come around for barbecues. When I examined her backyard, I found a patio littered with weatherbeaten furniture surrounded by tubs full of weeds. On my advice, she purchased new furniture and an attractive umbrella, and filled her tubs with glorious summer blooms. The atmosphere changed completely, and soon her friends were flocking around to see her.

Your Clutter Notebook

In this section of the book, you identify your personal clutter chaos by completing the questionnaires and sketching simple diagrams of your existing rooms.

First, fill in the questionnaires that are included on the Home, the Home Office, and the Yard/Garden, so that you can assess where you are overcrowded and where your junk is gathering, or what inner problems are holding you back from achieving your full potential. Next, study the sample diagrams for inside the home (see pages 152–161, 164–165) that indicate the likely places where piles of clutter gather and inhibit the positive flow of energy through your rooms. Now spend some time drawing in your own rooms on the graph pages provided, following the instructions with the diagrams, and see where your clutter hotspots are located. When you know where your problem areas exist, you can prioritize where to start clearing out, following the book's projects and adding in any that are specific to your home.

Drawing your plans

When you draw a plan of your hall or another room, it doesn't have to be to scale. Draw in the shape of the room and mark in the furniture and fittings you have there. Mark in bold with an "x" in red pen where clutter piles exist. Now draw in your first chi flow with a colored pen, starting at the door, indicating how it moves around the room in spirals until it exits by a window on the other side of the room. Then, using another colored pen, mark the chi energy coming back in the same window or one next to it, and show its flow around the room until it finally goes out through the door.

With the hall, show two chi flows coming through the door, one going up the stairs (if you have stairs) and the other continuing along the hall. You will now see clearly how your clutter piles are inhibiting the flow of energy around this area, and be able to identify where you need to take urgent action.

Is Your Clutter Taking Over?

Fill in this questionnaire to find out if clutter is taking over in your home.

YES **NO** **SOMETIMES**

1 Do you always feel overwhelmed by your clutter when you enter your home?
If your answer is yes, write down below the major items that are cluttering your hall:

❶ _____   **❷** _____
❸ _____   **❹** _____
❺ _____   **❻** _____
❼ _____   **❽** _____
❾ _____   **❿** _____

2 Are you irritated by the disorder in your home but unable to make a start on it?

3 Are you always buying items that you don't really need but just fancy buying?

4 Is your home full of possessions you have inherited?
If your answer is yes, write down below what they are:

❶ _____   **❷** _____
❸ _____   **❹** _____
❺ _____   **❻** _____
❼ _____   **❽** _____
❾ _____   **❿** _____

5 Do you hang onto useless equipment or possessions because you feel they may be useful sometime?

6 Are you quite organized but living with someone who can't throw anything away?

7 Can you easily find your keys and mobile phone each morning?

8 Is your attic a dumping ground for things you don't use, or items from your past?

9 Do you buy the latest exercise equipment but soon lose interest and leave them to fester?

10 Are your kids copying your hoarding habit and refusing to give away any of their toys?

11 Have you brought boxes from your old home that you still haven't opened?

12 Are there files lurking somewhere that contain bank or credit card statements that are more than five years old?

13 Do you still have some of your goods stored in your parents' attic?

14 Is your bedroom an overcrowded room that depresses you?
If your answer is yes, list the areas where you have clutter:

❶ _____   **❷** _____
❸ _____   **❹** _____
❺ _____   **❻** _____
❼ _____   **❽** _____
❾ _____   **❿** _____

15 Do you regularly throw out or give away the clothes you don't wear?

16 Is your bathroom really overcrowded with beauty and cleaning products?

17 Are you determined to get rid of all your junk, but feel frightened of losing its protection?

18 Are you depressed and lethargic because your home is such a mess?

YES NO SOMETIMES

19 Close your eyes and visualize how you would feel if one of your cluttered areas was cleared. Do you get a feeling of relief and satisfaction?

20 Now close your eyes and visualize your home as clean and ordered with good storage units. Does this make you feel more in control?

21 Do you have problems letting go of sentimental possessions?

If your answer is yes, list the type of possessions you have kept:

❶ _____   ❷ _____
❸ _____   ❹ _____
❺ _____   ❻ _____
❼ _____   ❽ _____
❾ _____   ❿ _____

22 Do you have a clear-out every six months to get rid of things you don't use?

23 Do you dispose of junk mail straight away, and open your mail daily to check statements or pay bills?

24 Is it normal for you to ask your family to clean up regularly?

25 Can you move around your living room easily?

If your answer is no, list what is taking up space in your living area:

❶ _____   ❷ _____
❸ _____   ❹ _____
❺ _____   ❻ _____
❼ _____   ❽ _____
❾ _____   ❿ _____

26 Are your videos and DVDs neatly stacked in a cabinet or rack?

27 Have you kept virtually every photograph you have taken?

28 Is it hard to see your kitchen counter tops because there is so much equipment on them?

If your answer is yes, write down what you have on your counter tops:

29 Do you let your trash can overflow before you empty it?

30 Do you have lots of different cookery books that you never use?

TOTAL SCORE

Score two points for a "Yes," one for a "Sometimes," and zero for a "No."

40–60
Clutter seems to be taking over in your home and affecting your moods, depleting your energy levels and inhibiting your progress. Take a long look at the areas that are causing you problems and immediately schedule in time to start decluttering, following the steps in the seven projects on pages 98–129. This is your path to a junk-free life.

20–39
You are not yet sinking under masses of clutter, but it is starting to irritate you. If you don't sort it now, it will only get worse and affect your home life. Focus on the worst areas, following the seven projects on pages 98–129.

19 and under
Clutter is not yet a problem, but it can grow easily, so get to grips with it now—before it starts to control you. Search for suspect corners, then follow the steps in the seven projects on pages 98–129, and deal with the junked-up areas.

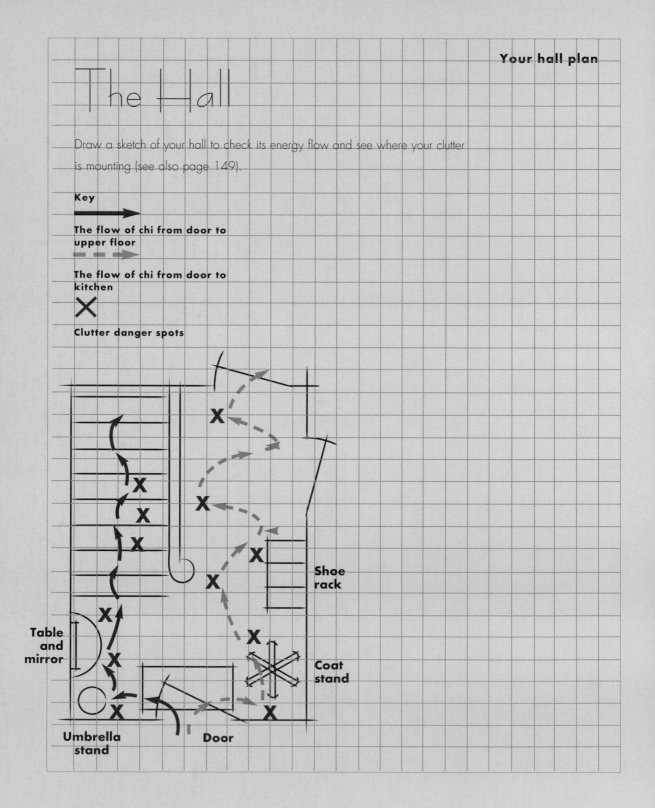

The Hall

Draw a sketch of your hall to check its energy flow and see where your clutter is mounting (see also page 149).

Key

The flow of chi from door to upper floor

The flow of chi from door to kitchen

Clutter danger spots

Shoe rack

Coat stand

Table and mirror

Umbrella stand

Door

The Kitchen

Draw a sketch of your kitchen, marking on its energy flow and to see where your clutter is mounting (see also pages 149 and 154).

The Living Room

Draw your living room following the example below, highlighting your clutter piles and chi flow (see also page 149).

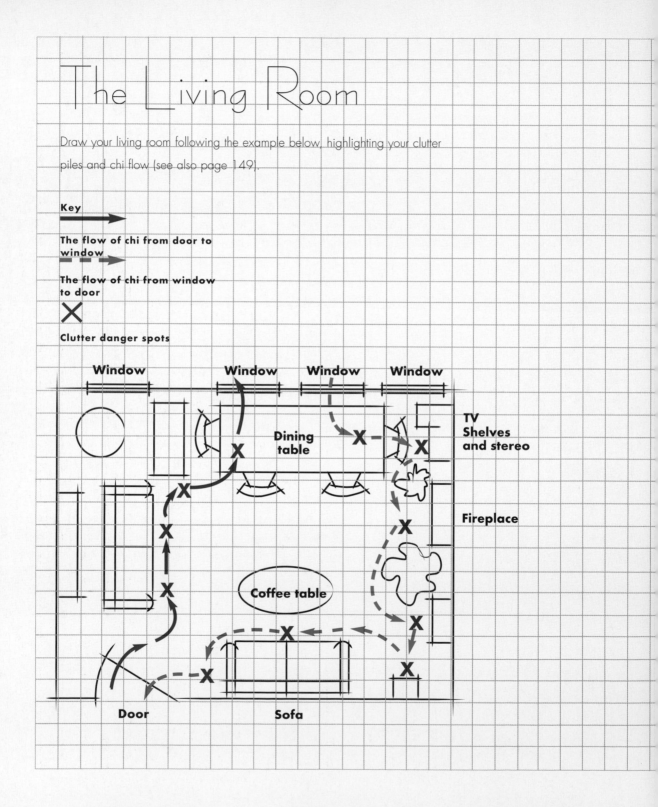

Key

The flow of chi from door to window

The flow of chi from window to door

✕

Clutter danger spots

Window   Window   Window   Window

Dining table

TV Shelves and stereo

Fireplace

Coffee table

Door   Sofa

Your living room plan

The Bedroom

Draw in your bedroom in the same style as the example below, and mark in your clutter piles and chi flow (see also pages 149 and 154).

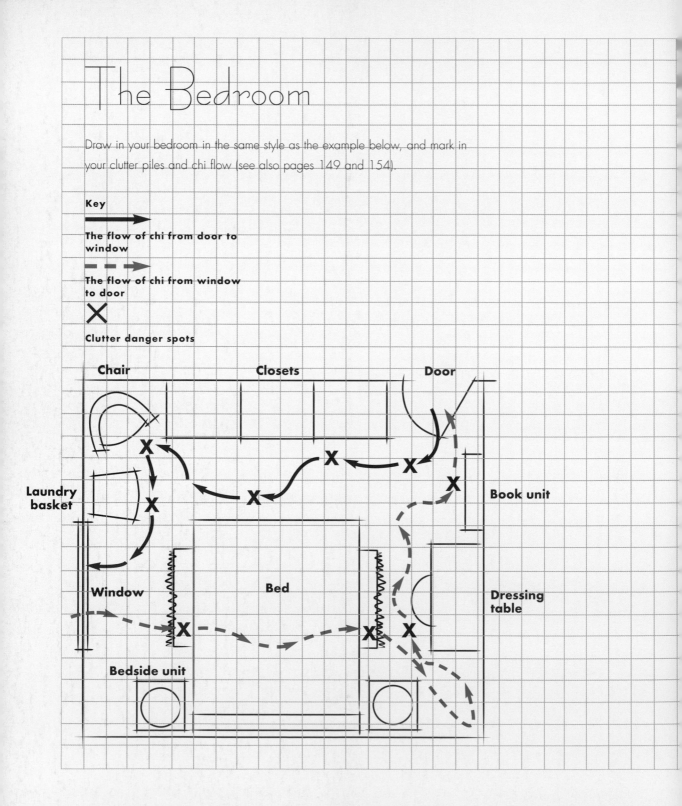

Key

The flow of chi from door to window

The flow of chi from window to door

Clutter danger spots

Your bedroom plan

The Child's Bedroom

Draw in your child's and guest bedrooms to see the energy flow and find out where the clutter lurks (see pages 149 and 154).

Key

⟶

The flow of chi from door to window

--- ⟶

The flow of chi from window to door

✕

Clutter danger spots

Your child's bedroom plan

The Bathroom

Draw in your bathroom plan as shown below, and highlight your clutter piles and the flow of chi (see also pages 149 and 154).

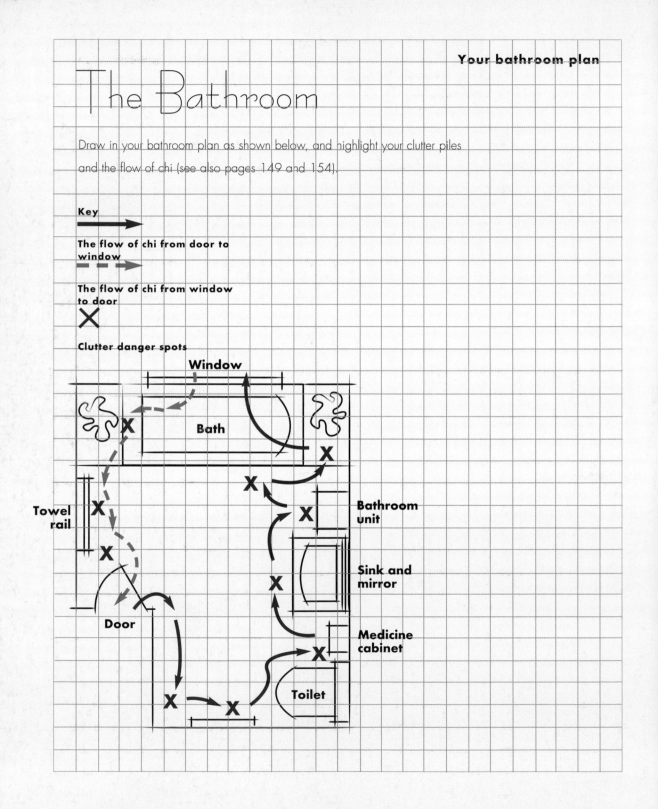

Key

The flow of chi from door to window

The flow of chi from window to door

Clutter danger spots

Window

Bath

Towel rail

Door

Bathroom unit

Sink and mirror

Medicine cabinet

Toilet

Your attic plan

The Attic Plan

Draw a plan of your attic to see what clutter piles are stopping the energy flow. Indicate only one flow of chi—show it coming through the door and circulating clockwise around the obstacles in the room and out of the door again (see pages 149 and 154).

Is Your Office a Clutter Dumping Ground?

Fill in this questionnaire to discover if you are working in a disaster zone.

YES   NO   SOMETIMES

1 Does your heart sink when you enter your workspace because there is so much stuff in it?

2 Is your job suffering because you are working in chaos?

3 Do you constantly suffer from headaches or feel tense that you work in such a mess?

4 If you shut your eyes and imagine your office as a neat, ordered place, does that make you feel better?

5 Is your office full of equipment and paperwork?

If your answer is yes, write below the equipment you have and what sort of paperwork:

1 _____   **2** _____
3 _____   **4** _____
5 _____   **6** _____
7 _____   **8** _____
9 _____   **10** _____

6 Is your idea of filing stacking piles of paper on the floor?

7 Are you storing equipment that has broken or doesn't work properly?

8 Do you always have an overflowing trash can?

9 Is your desk so littered with correspondence, files, and notes that you never know where to start work?

If your answer is yes, write down below what is on your desk at the moment:

1 _____   **2** _____
3 _____   **4** _____
5 _____   **6** _____
7 _____   **8** _____
9 _____   **10** _____

10 Do you try and leave your desk clear each evening?

11 If someone rings with a correspondence query, does it take you ages to find the relevant letter?

12 Do you have a regular weekly/monthly system for paying invoices?

13 Are you always tripping over piles of files and books around your desk?

If your answer is yes, write down what is surrounding your desk at the moment:

1 _____   **2** _____
3 _____   **4** _____
5 _____   **6** _____
7 _____   **8** _____
9 _____   **10** _____

14 Are you struggling to find current contact numbers because there are so many crossings out in your personal organizer?

15 Are your filing cabinets bulging with too much old material?

If your answer is yes, write down what sort of files they contain (current or redundant):

YES   NO   SOMETIMES

1 _____ **2** _____
3 _____ **4** _____
5 _____ **6** _____
7 _____ **8** _____
9 _____ **10** _____

16 Does your computer take ages to download files because the hard disk is too crowded?

17 Do you keep over 100 emails regularly in your inbox?

18 Are there programs on your computer that are out of date or that you never use?

If your answer is yes, list what they are:

1 _____ **2** _____
3 _____ **4** _____
5 _____ **6** _____
7 _____ **8** _____
9 _____ **10** _____

19 Is your office bulletin or pinboard full of out-of-date cards and contact numbers?

20 Do you have a stationery cabinet/drawer full of unused paper or broken or discarded equipment?

If your answer is yes, list what is in there:

1 _____ **2** _____
3 _____ **4** _____
5 _____ **6** _____
7 _____ **8** _____
9 _____ **10** _____

21 Do you keep lots of old reference books and magazines on your shelves?

22 Are you still storing accounts material from over fifteen years ago?

23 Is your printer malfunctioning, but you can never be bothered to get it fixed?

24 Do you have a "pending" file or inbox tray that rarely gets looked at?

25 Have you noticed that new work has dwindled since your office became messy?

TOTAL SCORE

Score two points for a "Yes," one for a "Sometimes," and zero for a "No."

35–50
Your office space is becoming out of control—and its disorder is affecting how you perform and your credibility in the workplace. Assess the worst areas to tackle and start on The Home Office Challenge steps (see pages 130–135) to bring the creativity back into your business life.

20–34
You are not buried under paperwork yet, but it is accumulating rapidly, so set up some processing systems before you lose the battle. Deal with your clutter black spots and follow The Home Office Challenge steps (see pages 130–135).

19 and under
Before you start to feel smug at your low score, remember clutter problems can easily sneak up on you. Re-organize any potential clutter hotspots, and follow any relevant steps in The Home Office Challenge (see pages 130–135).

The Home Office

Draw a plan of your home office as below, showing how your piles of clutter are affecting its flow of chi (see also pages 149 and 154).

Key

→ The flow of chi from door to window

⇢ The flow of chi from window to door

✗ Clutter danger spots

Window

Chair

Printer

Book and fax unit

Bin

Computer

Scanner

Filing cabinets

Shelves

Your home office plan

Is Your Yard/Garden a Total Mess?

Fill in this questionnaire to find out if your yard or garden is a chaotic mess.

YES   NO   SOMETIMES

1 Is the path leading to your door covered in moss, and are there broken slabs?

2 Do you struggle to reach your door because of the overgrown bushes and shrubs?

3 Does your heart sink as you walk into your chaotic yard or garden?

4 Visualize your perfect space with neat lawns, barbecue area, and flourishing borders—does that make you feel good?

5 Is your garden a dumping ground for unwanted goods?

If your answer is yes, detail what junk you have in your garden:

❶ _____   ❷ _____
❸ _____   ❹ _____
❺ _____   ❻ _____
❼ _____   ❽ _____
❾ _____   ❿ _____

6 Are you frightened to enter your overcrowded shed?

If your answer is yes, write down the major items in your shed:

❶ _____   ❷ _____
❸ _____   ❹ _____
❺ _____   ❻ _____
❼ _____   ❽ _____
❾ _____   ❿ _____

7 Do your garden tools have layers of rust?

8 Are you ashamed to invite people into your yard or garden?

9 When you look out on your front and back spaces, are they choking with weeds?

10 Do you let the grass grow up to knee height before you think of cutting it?

11 Are many parts of your yard or garden broken or decaying?

If your answer is yes, write down what they are:

❶ _____   ❷ _____
❸ _____   ❹ _____
❺ _____   ❻ _____
❼ _____   ❽ _____
❾ _____   ❿ _____

12 Do you never invite friends to a barbecue because your back space is an eyesore?

13 Do your drains constantly get blocked up?

14 Do you have lots of cracked terra-cotta pots stacked up out the back?

15 Do you feel insecure because the fence between your house and your neighbors' is falling down?

16 Do you still have builders' debris left from months or years ago?

YES   NO   SOMETIMES

17 If you have a pond, has it been neglected?

If your answer is yes, write down what it now contains:

1 _____   **2** _____

3 _____   **4** _____

5 _____   **6** _____

7 _____   **8** _____

9 _____   **10** _____

18 Have your plants or vegetables been badly attacked by garden pests?

19 Do you regularly dump old refrigerators, washing machines, or other equipment in your yard or garden?

20 Have you lost your garden hose or is your watering can broken?

21 Do you often leave dead flowers unattended, or have piles of dead leaves around?

22 Is much of your garden furniture broken, badly stained, or unusable?

If your answer is yes, detail what is wrong with it:

1 _____   **2** _____

3 _____   **4** _____

5 _____   **6** _____

7 _____   **8** _____

9 _____   **10** _____

23 Do tradespeople keep complaining to you about your broken gate?

24 Are you always planning to work on the yard or garden, but never seem to make a start?

25 Do you have any rotting or decaying trees?

TOTAL SCORE

Score two points for a "Yes," one for a "Sometimes," and zero for a "No."

35–50
You are in danger of not finding the way into your yard or garden or beating the path to your shed. You will drain your energy and could become discouraged if you leave the area like this, so make a list of your priority hotspots to deal with and start on the Yard/Garden projects' steps on pages 136–147 to restore some harmony and balance in this bountiful space.

20–34
Your yard or garden is not a complete mess of weeds or decaying vegetation, but it is well on its way. Nip it in the bud by working on your worst areas; go through the Yard/Garden steps on pages 136–147.

19 and under
Praise yourself for your low score, but don't become complacent. Your yard or garden may seem a haven now, but a few rainy days can turn it into a jungle—so attend to your worst spots and complete any of the appropriate steps in the Yard/Garden projects on pages 136–147.

The Front Yard and Backyard/Garden

Draw in plans of both your front yard and backyard or garden. For each plan, in the same way as the attic, just draw one chi flow from the door going around the yard in a circular route until it exits via the same door (see page 161). Mark in all clutter, including overgrown shrubs, weeds, decaying trees, stagnant ponds, and broken flowerpots.

Key

→

The flow of chi from the door, around the yard

✗

Clutter danger spots

Your front yard/garden plan

Your backyard/garden plan

Index

Acknowledgments

I would like to thank Cindy Richards for her patience and input in forwarding this book project, and Liz Dean for her friendship, flair, creative input, and usual efficient organization in editing and running this book. Also thanks to Paul Wood and Roger Daniels for their design skills and Trina Dalziel, Sam Wilson, and Kate Simunek for their attractive illustrations. My appreciation also goes to my feng shui master Harrison Kyng for setting me off on the wonderful path of feng shui. Finally a big hug to my sister Cill for her ongoing encouragement and thanks to all my friends particularly Claire, Ann, Cathy, Lynne, Sarah, and Steve who as ever supported me through the writing process.

Mary Lambert is based in London and can be contacted for feng shui and clutter-clearing consultations for homes and businesses via email: marylambert@f2s.com

www.marylambertfengshui.com

Picture Credits

The publishers are grateful to the following for permission to reproduce photographs:

pp 2, 104, 105, 106, 111, 115, 148: With thanks to Sainsbury's Home; designed to inspire, this stylish, practical, and affordable range enhances your home (www.sainsburys.co.uk);
p8: Polly Wreford/Abigail Ahern's home in London (Atelier Abigail Ahern www.atelierabigailahern.com)
p 9: Christopher Drake/A house designed by Artist Angela A'Court, extension and alteration to rear of property by S.I. Robertson at 23 Architecture (Angela A'Court—orangedawe@hotmail.com/S.I. Robertson at 23 Architecture-www.23arc.com)
pp 11, 39 below right, 42 below, 61 left, 70, 74 left and right, 85: The Holding Company;
pp 13, 23, 68, 89: Neo Vision/Photonica;
p 15 above: Pia Tryde/The General Trading Company;
pp 15 below, 58, 62: Henry Wilson/Interior Archive.
pp 17, 27, 85 above right: GettyOne Stone;
p 18: Michael Crockett/www.ewastock.com;
pp 21, 42 above, 44 right: Simon Brown/Interior Archive;
p 22: Crabtree & Evelyn;
p 25 above and below: Jacqui Hurst;
p 29: Karin Taylor/Marie Claire/IPC Syndication;
pp 32, 54, 88, 91: Feng Shui for Modern Living/Centennial Publishing;
pp 34, 37, 61 right, 65, 94, 95: The Pier;
pp 36, 56, 67: Fritz von der Schulenburg/Interior Archive;
pp 39: above, 44 left, 60, 61 center, 64, 71, 72, 81 below: The Cotswold Company;
pp 41 above and below, 43, 45: Abode UK;
p 46: Tim Beddow/Interior Archive;
p 48: Nadia Mackenzie/Interior Archive;

p 50: www.ewastock.com;
p 51: Tom Leighton/www.ewastock.com;
p 53: Michael Dunne/www.ewastock.com;
p 55: Laurence Dutton/The General Trading Company;
pp 59 and 78: Rodney Hyett/www.ewastock.com;
p 66 above and below: The White Company;
pp 73, 75, 79, 81 above: Muji;
p 80: Josie Clyde/Stock Shot;
p 83: Pictor International;
p 84: Peugeot;
p 86: Osprey by Graeme Ellisdon;
p 87 below left: Filofax;
p 90: David Giles/www.ewastock.com;
p 92: T. Sawada/Photonica;
p 93: Michael Nicholson/www.ewastock.com;
p 97: Polly Wreford/Charlotte-Anne Fidler's home in London
p 99: Mark Luscombe-Whyte/www.ewastock.com;
p 103: Neil Davis/www.ewastock.com;
p 109: Tom Leighton/www.ewastock.com;
pp 119, 145: The White Company—suppliers of fine linens and accessories for the home (+44 (0)870 9009555, www.thewhiteco.com);
p 123: Bruce Hemming/www.ewastock.com;
p 127: Lu Jeffery/www.elizabethwhiting.com;
p 128: 4 My Way of Life—handmade paper boxes are made entirely from renewable and recycled ingredients noted for their natural texture (+44 (0)870 241 5471, www.4mywayoflife.com);
p 131: Tom Leighton/www.ewastock.com;
p 137: Ian Parry/www.ewastock.com;
p 139: Tim Street-Porter/www.ewastock.com;
p 140: Tino Tedaldi;
p 143: Dennis Stone/www.ewastock.com.

Wish card